ROMAN POTTERY

A. *Jar (Form 72) with applied moulded and slip decoration. Found at Felixstowe. Probably Lezoux. Late 2nd century* A.D. *Ht.* 7¾ *in. British Museum (B. & M.). See page* 19

ROMAN POTTERY

by

R. J. CHARLESTON
of the Victoria and Albert Museum

FABER AND FABER
24 Russell Square
London

738·30937
CHA

First published in mcmlv
by Faber and Faber Limited
24 Russell Square London W.C.1
Printed in Great Britain by
R. MacLehose and Company Limited
The University Press Glasgow
Blocks made and colour plates printed by
Fine Art Engravers Limited, Esher

To

W. B. HONEY

with gratitude and affection

FOREWORD

Mr. Charleston's book is the first in English to deal in a comprehensive way with a subject which has hitherto attracted little attention. It may be argued that it is not one subject but many; that there is no more a Roman pottery style than a British style of the same period. The export trade prevailing at the time, especially in the 'red-gloss' wares, has tended to obscure this. But there were many Roman provincial types sustained by local tradition and well worth the scholar's attention. It has been no light task to gather the threads, but one well worth while and likely to be valuable to many local archaeologists as well as to connoisseurs.

The book is illustrated by a hundred plates (of which four are in colour), chosen throughout for their aesthetic merit, and ranging from the widely popular 'red-gloss' wares, the so-called Arretine and 'Samian' wares and their kindred, to the attractive Alexandrian green-glazed wares and other Egypto-Roman types.

W. B. H.

FOREWORD

CONTENTS

ILLUSTRATIONS

xi

ILLUSTRATIONS

ILLUSTRATIONS

ACKNOWLEDGEMENTS

The author wishes to express his indebtedness to many colleagues and friends who have helped him with advice and information, and, in particular, to Miss Kathleen M. Kenyon, of the Institute of Archaeology, University of London; Dr. P. Corder, of the Society of Antiquaries of London; Dr. D. B. Harden, of the Ashmolean Museum, Oxford; Mr. E. M. Jope, of the Department of Archaeology, Queen's University, Belfast; and Mr. E. A. Lane, Keeper of the Department of Ceramics, Victoria and Albert Museum, who have read his manuscript, in part or in whole, and have made valuable suggestions and criticisms.

The following Museums or Institutes have kindly authorized publication of photographs of objects in their collections: Staatlichen Museen, Berlin; Rheinisches Landesmuseum, Bonn; Museum of Fine Arts, Boston; University Museum of Archaeology and Ethnology, Cambridge; Colchester and Essex Museum, Colchester; Römisch-Germanisches Museum, Cologne; Eton College Museum; Museum für Kunst und Gewerbe, Hamburg; Palestine Archaeological Museum, Jerusalem; Rijksmuseum van Oudheden, Leyden; British Museum,[1] the Joint Expedition to Samaria, and Victoria and Albert Museum, London; Römisch-Germanisches Zentralmuseum, Mainz; Hispanic Society of America and Metropolitan Museum of Art, New York; Ashmolean Museum, Oxford; Cabinet des Médailles, Bibliothèque Nationale, and Musée du Louvre, Paris; Reading Museum; Vatican Museum, Rome; Royal Ontario Museum of Archaeology, Toronto; Landesmuseum, Trier; Yale University Art Gallery; Yorkshire Museum, York.

[1] The Department of Greek and Roman Antiquities is designated 'G. and R.' in the captions to the Plates, and the Department of British and Medieval Antiquities 'B. and M.'.

1

INTRODUCTION

'Maior pars hominum terrenis utitur vasis'[1]

'Roman vases are far inferior in nearly all respects to Greek; the shapes are less artistic, and the decoration, though not without merits of its own, bears the same relation to that of Greek vases that all Roman art does to Greek art. . . . Roman vases, in a word, require only the skill of the potter for their completion, and the processes employed are largely mechanical. . . .' These sentiments, expressed by H. B. Walters in his *History of Ancient Pottery*, published in 1905, have a convincing tone of finality, and would probably be accepted by most people as a fair appraisal of values. At the time when they were written they must have seemed unquestionably right. The taut and disciplined forms of Greek pottery of the best period; the superb painting, so vitally executed and so consummately ordered both in its internal values and in its relationship to the vase on which it stands—what could surpass these? In their own kind, nothing. These values seem indeed immutable. But since Walters wrote, both art history and the appreciation of pottery have extended the horizons of their sympathy. The school of art historians chiefly associated with the name of Josef Strzygowsky has gained general acceptance for the view that the 'un-classical' elements in Hellenistic and Roman art are not necessarily due to 'debasement' or 'degeneration', but may reveal the impact on classical art of other cultures with divergent, but nonetheless positive, values of their own. Secondly, in the history of ceramic appreciation, we have witnessed in the past thirty years the ascendancy and supremacy of the Chinese pottery and porcelain made before the Ming dynasty. We have learned that softness of form has charms not less than those of a metallic profile; that freedom, and even wildness, may vie with discipline in painting; that the brush is not the only instrument proper for decorating a pot; and that the colours and surface-qualities of glazes offer infinite possibilities of delight. The sensuous has taken its place beside the intellectual in the scale of values. It may be suspected that the tendency has been carried too

[1] Pliny, *Natural History*, Book XXXV, 12 (46) 160.

far, but wherever the true balance lies, fresh sensibilities have been awakened, from which Roman pottery should evoke many responses.

Not only is much Roman pottery not 'less artistic' than Greek in the basic excellence of form, but there existed under the Roman Empire a diversity of decorative techniques unexplored in classical Greece. The plasticity of clay beneath the potter's hand was exploited not only in the throwing of the pot (and a thrown vessel can have other charms than a lathe-produced accuracy) but in the incising or impressing of decorative *motifs*, or the squeezing or rolling of clay embellishments. Not least, clay in a semi-liquid state was poured on in that 'slip' technique which is one of the glories of simple pottery, and which exacts a discipline parallel to that of painting and, in its way, hardly less demanding. Painting itself was practised, but in a technique different from that of Greek pottery and with no comparable pretensions: nevertheless, a taste attuned to the powerful and eloquent formalism of the painting on the Chinese stonewares of Tzŭ-Chou, will probably take readily enough to the painted pottery of Nabataea or Nubia.

To speak of 'Roman pottery' at all is in a sense to create a false entity. The Roman Empire embraced in its political structure almost as many and diverse cultures as the British, and some had characteristic and original contributions to make in the field of ceramics. Egypt and the Near East, for instance, brought with their glazing techniques a wealth of colour previously undreamed of, or perhaps consciously rejected, in the indigenous pottery of the Greco-Roman world. In a contrary movement, however, to these innovations from the periphery, may be observed the diffusion outwards of a central tradition. This tradition has both its technical and its formal characteristics, not always inextricably combined. The technique of imparting a gloss (usually black or red) to pottery was inherited from the Greeks and passed on to the marginal territories of the Empire, there sometimes to invest barbaric forms. Contrariwise, a feeling for form which apparently sprang from the soil of the nuclear countries of the Empire appears to have stimulated an immediate response on the periphery, where Italian or Gaulish shapes might be imitated in the local ceramic material. This central tradition is discussed in the first chapter of the present book.

No clear line, however, can be drawn between the products of the central tradition and those of the marginal lands, either technically or in terms of artistic development: for the 'gloss' technique of surface-treatment may degenerate by infinitesimal gradations which permit of no clear line of demarcation, and forms are susceptible of equally subtle perversions. There are some types of pots, therefore, which might almost as well figure in the first chapter as amongst the 'coarse' wares of the last. Whereas in the one, however, there is an organic development which imposes its own logic and coherence, the other is of necessity a catalogue of diverse types. The possible claimants for inclusion in such an assemblage are numberless, and in a book of this scope it has only been feasible to admit those which pleaded aesthetic, and not historic, grounds for admission.

If the diffusive power of a 'civilized' central tradition and the reactions which it provokes in less 'civilized' provinces are matters which cannot be explained by oversimplification, it is certain that political ascendancy and social superiority are potent factors in the process. But if the power and wealth of Rome helped the spread of Greco-Roman culture in 'backward' provinces, in Egypt and the Near East there existed already a wealthy hellenized civilization which was perhaps less impressionable.

In these lands there flourished separate traditions of colour-glazed pottery which trace their origins to the remote antiquity of Babylonia on the one hand, and of early dynastic Egypt on the other. This pottery is the subject of Chapter 2. It is distinct from all other pottery of the Roman period in that it was coated with a true vitreous glaze of the type universally familiar in the modern world. Yet it, too, was ultimately absorbed into the general stream, for lead-glazing spread to Italy, Gaul and even further afield in the northern barbarian provinces, to reappear finally, after vicissitudes as yet not known, as the lead-glazed pottery of medieval Europe.

The only inclusive books which have hitherto been written on Roman pottery have been in the nature of handbooks or catalogues of large museum collections, with the exception of that part of Walters' *History of Ancient Pottery* which deals with Roman wares and from which the quotation prefacing this Introduction was taken: this account, however, ignores many of the wares which have recommended themselves in the present book. In general, Roman pottery has been the province of the archaeologist, for whom the indestructibility of pottery has made it the most reliable, because ever-present, medium of fixing chronology. Since Roman archaeology is almost inevitably conducted within provincial compartments, specialization is the order of the day, and the excavator of Roman Britain is likely to be somewhat at sea in dealing with finds from, for example, Roman North Africa. Such specialists, strongly entrenched, and able to use their chosen pottery as a refined instrument in fixing dates, may find cause for complaint in the sections of this book which are devoted to their speciality, or from which perhaps it has been omitted.[1] The apology must be that the book was not written primarily for them, and that in it chronology has been subordinated to aesthetic considerations.

[1] Lamps, figurines and tiles have, except for one or two isolated instances, been expressly excluded.

2

RED-GLOSS POTTERY

Vasari, in his *Lives of the Painters*, records that his grandfather, Giorgio Vasari, presented Lorenzo de' Medici, on the occasion of a visit to Arezzo, with four complete vases which had been dug out in a field near the town. This gift was deemed to have secured to the family the favour of the Medici. Arezzo was anciently Arretium, and the vases in question were of that glossy red 'Arretine' ware which for many people has come to symbolize the essential qualities of Roman pottery. This is a drastic oversimplification, but there is a large element of truth in it, for the red-gloss pottery was not only the most widely dispersed single type of ware in the Roman world, but was virtually peculiar to it; and of all the fabrics of this pottery, the Arretine was artistically the most ambitious and successful. A certain Ser Ristoro d'Arezzo has recorded for posterity the finding of some pottery fragments in his native town towards the end of the thirteenth century. 'When any of these fragments come into the hands of sculptors or artists or other connoisseurs,' he writes, 'they consider them like sacred relics, marvelling that human nature could rise to such a height in the subtlety, in the workmanship, and the form of those vases, and in their colours and their figures in relief; and they say that the makers were divine or the vases fell from heaven.' Pottery which was regarded with such enthusiasm by Italians both of the Early and of the High Renaissance has claims on anybody's attention, and this chapter must be regarded as a crescendo and a diminuendo, at the climax of which lies Arretine pottery. First, however, should be examined the feature which, in different forms and to varying degrees of perfection, is common to all the wares of this family, whether decorated in relief or left plain.

The method of procuring the gloss on Roman red wares was for long a mystery. The cumulative researches of scholars who have concerned themselves with the techniques of Greek vase-painting (the red colour and general gloss of which are so obviously akin to those of the Roman wares) have at last satisfactorily solved the problem. The culminating study—that of Dr. Thomas Schumann published during the late War[1]—has, by a series of inferences and controlling

[1] See Bibliography.

5

experiments, demonstrated that the Greek potters, in producing the fine even glossy surface on their wares, merely exploited certain of the material characteristics of clay. The minute particles of which clay is composed, often of sub-microscopic size, have a natural tendency to coagulate under the influence of forces of an electrical and gravitational nature. If, however, a small quantity of alkaline solution is added to a clay-and-water mixture, it counteracts the mutual electrical attraction of the clay crystals, and the particles float in a more or less free suspension in the water. This is known as 'peptization' and is analogous to the processes of digestion. If a mixture of the kind described is allowed to stand a while, the larger clay particles and various impurities tend to sink to the bottom of the vessel in which they are contained. In consequence, the liquid at the top of the vessel consists of the finest clay particles in suspension in water. If a pot is dipped in this liquid and then fired, a fine film of tiny clay particles is deposited all over its surface. This film reflects light in a manner reminiscent of the fibres of silk. The red colour is the result of using an iron-bearing clay and firing it in a clear flame in the kiln. This 'oxydizing' atmosphere leaves unaffected the red ferric oxide in the clay.

Near Eastern Forerunners

Isolated examples of red gloss make their appearance in Athens as early as the sixth century B.C., and red and black often appear together on undecorated vessels in the two subsequent centuries and in Hellenistic times. The same dichromatic feature occurs (although owing to the rarity of its occurrence, it may be considered an accident of firing) on fragments of the earliest red-gloss ware to have been identified as a definite and distinct fabric.

This ware is distinguished as 'PERGAMENE' pottery, owing to the historical accident that the first writer to isolate it associated it with the most eminent city in a list of Asia Minor pottery-centres enumerated by the Roman author Pliny. That it was not made at Pergamum now seems almost certain, although the name, distinguished by inverted commas, must serve until a better is found. It has been met with in varying quantities on excavated sites in Greece and the Aegean, Asia Minor, Palestine and Syria, Egypt and North Africa, and Cyprus. This distribution suggests that 'Pergamene' pottery was made at some centre with easy access to the sea, situated at the Eastern end of the Mediterranean. The presence, on some pieces, of stamped representations of the headdress of the Egyptian goddess Isis suggests that Alexandria may, in fact, have been a seat of manufacture; but it is possible that closely similar pottery was made at more than one centre.

'Pergamene' pottery is characterized by a buffish body, varying considerably in hardness and colour, and a dark-red non-porous gloss of indifferent sheen. In Hellenistic times it comprised in the main large plates, bowls, and cups. The decoration of these pots is almost entirely impressed or incised, although a few moulded fragments have been found. The normal scheme for the open bowls and plates is contained within two series of incised or rouletted concentric circles, the inner one enclosing an impressed rosette, the outer forming with the inner a frieze in which are radially disposed impressed palmette-forms (1) or the 'headdress of Isis' already referred to above.

Examples of 'Pergamene' ware datable to the first half of the first century B.C. have been found in both Greece and the Near East, and the repertory of shapes indicated above seems to have lasted from then until at least the very end of the same century, when a new spirit makes itself felt. It is impossible, on the strength of the evidence at present available, to be sure to what extent, at this point, Arretine pottery (see pp. 11 ff. below) directly influenced the wares of the Eastern Mediterranean, and to what extent both shared a common sense of form current at that moment. It seems fairly certain, however, that Arretine pottery, in its fully developed form and at the height of its repute, exercised a very powerful influence on the potters of other lands, who were stimulated to competition and therefore to imitation. The supremacy of Arretine ware was no doubt due to its superior surface qualities, but the effect of this supremacy was to modify the shapes of rival wares and not their technical characteristics. That this policy of imitation proved successful is indicated by the fact that the importation of Arretine wares into the Eastern Mediterranean seems hardly to extend beyond the limits of the Augustan period, after which the local pottery, emerging from its metamorphosis, reasserted itself.

The fabric of 'Pergamene' pottery during this early Roman phase, although distinct, does not differ markedly from what preceded it, and shows similarly wide variations of body and gloss. This is well demonstrated by two fragments found at Antioch, differing in body and surface-colour, but both marked with the same potter's stamp. The characteristic forms of this phase are cups and plates (2). The cups are of three types, all roughly paralleled in Arretine pottery—one with a flaring, slightly concave, profile (3), the second with a double-ogee outline (4), the third resembling the first, but with a vertical lip (5). Potters' stamps (6) begin to make their appearance on these wares in about the first quarter of the first century A.D.

---

(1) *Plate* 1; (2) *Plate* 25B; (3) cf. *Plate* 10A; (4) cf. *Plate* 11A; (5) *Plate* 9A, cf. *Plate* 8A; (6) cf. *Plate* 25B.

In 'Pergamene' pottery, therefore, may be traced the earliest exclusive use of red gloss, and a possible source of this technical characteristic of Arretine pottery. Before passing on to the origin of the other salient characteristic of that pottery—the use of relief-decoration—it will be convenient to examine two other types of red-gloss pottery used in the Eastern Mediterranean, the first of which at least may antedate Arretine.

In the thirty-fifth Book of his *Natural History*,[1] which was dedicated in 77 A.D., Pliny writes: 'The greater part of mankind uses earthenware. The SAMIAN is to this day appreciated as a table-ware.' The word 'Samian' is used in association with the names of other places such as Arretium, a known pottery-centre; and the geographical context makes it certain that here the word can only mean 'of Samos'. As early as the second century B.C., however (as, for example, in the plays of Plautus), 'Samian' is clearly used in the generic sense of 'made of clay', and the wares so called therefore contrasted, in their simplicity and cheapness, with those of other more precious materials. The wording of Pliny's notice implies that the manufacture had been long established in Samos, and the older references suggest that, even as early as the second century B.C., the wares of Samos were so familiar in Italy that the word 'Samian' became synonymous with 'clay'. When, therefore, in the excavation of the Asia Minor town-site of Priene, pottery of a distinctive type was brought to light in considerable quantity, it was associated with the ware mentioned by Pliny. The proximity of Priene to Samos made the equation an attractive one, but it has as yet never been satisfactorily established.

This pottery is distinguished by a cinnamon-coloured or pinkish-yellow body full of particles of mica, and by a light orange-red gloss, which absorbs water. It has been recognized on sites in Greece, Syria, South Russia and Palestine, and in greater quantity on Samos itself. Unfortunately, none of the pieces known can be accurately dated on stratigraphical grounds, and analogies of shape with Arretine pottery have suggested that they belong to the Augustan and Tiberian periods (27 B.C.–A.D. 37). Moreover, the presence on certain pieces of what appears to be a misunderstood Latin potter's name suggests that Italian business enterprise, and even Italian potters, were penetrating this centre of the pottery industry, wherever it was in fact situated. This apparent dominance of Italy could hardly antedate the emergence of Arretium, and this emergence itself cannot be admitted to have taken place much before the third decade B.C. (see pp. 11–12 below). It is, however, by no means established that 'Samian' ware did not exist earlier than the first century B.C., and the presence on a number of red-gloss pieces of a stamp which, in a fragmentary form, also appears

[1] Book XXXV, 12 (46), 160.

to be used on a black-gloss dish, suggests that there was a continuity of manufacture extending back possibly to the second century B.C. However that may be, whether it was or was not an Eastern forerunner of red-gloss pottery in Italy, this 'Samian' appears to be a distinct fabric, with a physical character of its own and certain traits of manufacture more or less peculiar to itself. Among these may be reckoned a tendency to employ a low footrim, and the use for decorative purposes of stamped rosettes and rudimentary handles in the form of an S-shaped coil. The stamps used were either potters' names, usually Greek, or complimentary mottoes such as

ΚΕΡΔΟΣ

These were normally impressed within a rectangular frame, but on later types the shape was changed to the foot-sole familiar on the pottery of the Western parts of the Empire.[1]

That micaceous clay was not a peculiarity of the 'Samian' ware is shown by finds made elsewhere in the Near East. At TSCHANDARLI (probably the ancient Pitani), some thirty kilometres from Pergamum, in Asia Minor, masses of red-gloss pottery sherds, including wasters, have been excavated, clearly indicating the presence of a kiln in the vicinity. The vast majority were plain wheel-turned wares, but one or two finds of relief-decorated fragments, and the presence on or near the site of a mould and a relief with erotic subjects of a type familiar from the excavations of Pergamum, suggest that relief-decorated wares also were made in these or neighbouring kilns. Since, however, to judge by their shapes, the earliest wares at Tschandarli are of Tiberian date, the origins of Arretine relief-ware must be looked for in other quarters.

The majority of the early wares described so far were decorated, if at all, with incised or impressed patterns, and it remains to be considered where the method of ornamenting pottery by means of reliefs originated.

Ever since at least the end of the third century B.C. the Hellenized countries of the Eastern Mediterranean and the Aegean had been familiar with the moulded bowls now commonly and erroneously known as 'MEGARIAN' BOWLS. By a process which is instructive when we consider the organization of the later pottery-industry in Roman times, the manufacture of these moulded bowls appears to have spread —after being popularized in one or two great centres such as Alexandria—virtually all over the Hellenistic world. Thus, moulds for making them have been found at Antioch and at Delos, and it is virtually certain that they were also made in such scattered localities as Olbia or Panticapaeum in South Russia, at Sparta in the Peloponnese,

[1]The term 'Samian' has been loosely used of much red-gloss pottery found in the West. It is not so used in this book.

in Syria and in Alexandria. Fragments are found on almost all Hellenistic sites, and the probability is that they were also manufactured in a great many local potteries other than those mentioned.

The 'Megarian' bowls, although displaying a great variety in the qualities of clay and the disposition of the ornaments used, have certain characteristics in common which are relevant to their study as the forerunners of Roman relief-decorated pottery. They were made by pressing clay into a mould which had itself been decorated by means of separate stamps and occasionally of rouletted designs such as an *ovolo* border (cf. pp. 13–14 below). Sometimes the ornamentation of the base of a bowl included the name of the potter stamped in relief. When shaped, the bowls were fired, either in a reducing atmosphere to produce the black surface which, in the early phases of Hellenistic pottery, seems to have represented the most acceptable approximation to metalwork, or in an oxydizing atmosphere to produce red, a colour which, after tentative or perhaps accidental origins, finally triumphed over black in the course of the second and first centuries B.C. The ornamentation of these bowls, which commonly have a calyx of gadroons or of leaf-fronds rising from the base, is clearly derived from metalwork, and silver bowls of this general type have been found in, for example, the treasures of Nihavand, in Persia, and of Toukh el Qarmous, in Lower Egypt. To this basic pattern, however, were added natural and figural elements of all sorts (I).

Italy

It is well known that in Italy, during the fourth century B.C., the demand for painted pottery of Greek type ceased to be satisfied by importations from the Greek mainland, and was met to a far greater extent than previously by local production. This seems also to have occurred later in the case of relief-decorated pottery inspired by metal prototypes. Thus, at Cales in Campania were made black wares of open shapes, decorated with internal reliefs. Related wares were made probably at Pergamum and other Near Eastern centres, and probably derived ultimately from Pergamene toreutics. Similarly, bowls closely resembling the 'Megarian' bowls, but bearing the signatures of potters with Italian names written in Latin script, have been found in various parts of Italy, and were certainly made there. Thus the potter C. Popilius (or perhaps C. Popilius Cilo) adds to his signature the names alternatively of Mevania or Ocriculum, both towns in Umbria, while the signature of the potter L. Appius (or perhaps Lappius) is found both on one of the bowls of this class and on a cup belonging to

(I) *Plate* 2.

the Calene group mentioned above. The similarities between the bowls of this group (they followed in general the same formula in ornamentation) are such as to suggest that they were made in a more or less restricted area, probably in Umbria and Southern Etruria (1). Their manufacture appears to fall between the third century and the middle of the first century B.C., a period roughly coterminous with the duration of the 'Megarian' bowls further east. It is most likely, however, that they were made in the course of the first century B.C. Not very many examples have been found, and production cannot have been on a large scale. The scarcity of specimens contrasts strongly with the abundance of known Arretine wares, the manufacture of which lasted barely a hundred years.

It has been shown above that both the red-gloss technique and the use of impressed moulds were known in the Eastern Mediterranean at least as early as the second century B.C., and it has been suggested that these were the technical roots from which sprang ARRETINE pottery. 'Sprang' is hardly too violent a word to use, for Arretine pottery enjoyed a mushroom growth and as quickly died away, being superseded by provincial wares far less significant artistically, but possessed of the secret of economic vitality. The manufacture of red Arretine ware scarcely exceeded the period 30 B.C. to A.D. 30, with a possible extension during which a degenerate pottery continued to be made. Before the red-gloss phase, however, black-gloss wares were made at Arretium, and the continuity of work in the potteries there is shown by the fact that name-stamps which occur on the black ware recur later on the red. The former has been found in tombs at Rome from which the latter is absent, and these are dated to the early first century B.C. The process of transition was complete by about 25 B.C., when the moulded pottery first makes its appearance, and it may be presumed that an intervening period of uncertain duration was devoted to the production of plain red wares. The black pottery is often stamped with Greek slave-names in Latin characters, and it is difficult to resist the conclusion that, already at this stage, the pottery industry of Arretium was absorbing skilled potters who had been enslaved in the Roman campaigns in the East under Lucullus and Pompey, and who might have brought with them the secret of the red-gloss technique. It is more likely, however, that this change evidenced not so much the spread of a technical secret— which a relatively slight mischance in firing might suggest—as of a taste for red which began in the East and finally dominated the whole Roman world. In the case of red-gloss pottery with moulded reliefs,

---

(1) *Plate* 3.

however, the situation seems somewhat different. It appears to spring into existence complete in the perfection both of its physical and of its artistic qualities. It is possible to look at what is both the earliest and the finest Arretine ware—the first products of the firm of Perennius (1)—and to see in them the descendants of Calenian pottery or of the Umbrian relief-decorated bowls mentioned above, but it is not so easy to see what pottery may have filled out the intervening gaps in the pedigree, for that the one should have developed *direct* from the other is unthinkable. It is far easier to envisage Arretine relief-pottery as something abruptly introduced into a centre which had been shrewdly conceived as offering it the greatest economic scope. The pottery tradition was there, as also the commercial advantage in a world whose centre of power, economic as well as political, had, by the victory at Actium (31 B.C.), been shifted overnight from East to West. With this supposition the known facts accord well enough. The earliest datable Arretine relief-ware from excavations in Germany cannot have reached there before 15 B.C., and it does not include any of the earliest Perennius wares, which must therefore be considered to antedate 15 B.C. by at least some few years. The resemblance in style between the earlier and the later work of this firm, however, does not admit of too long a span, and the fall of Alexandria in 30 B.C. may be regarded as the event which provided for Arretium the pre-condition for its rapid development. There is, furthermore, one bowl by the earliest of the Perennius factory's slave-artists which bears an inscription apparently relating to the dedication in 29 B.C. of the rebuilt temple of Hercules Musarum in Rome. It is probable that the bowl was made while the memory of this event was still fresh.

A study of the potters' stamps has revealed that the first moving spirit in the Perennius enterprise was one Tigranus, freedman of Marcus Perennius. The name Tigranus is an Oriental one, borne by the kings of Armenia, and the artists' names within the same concern are Greek. It seems possible, therefore, that Marcus Perennius Tigranus, who was probably a business-man and company-promoter as much as a working potter, brought his team of Oriental Greek potters to Arretium between 30 and 25 B.C. The tradition in which he worked is to be sought in the East, probably in the regions of Asia Minor or Syria, and the techniques employed may now be described in detail.

The plain wares were simply thrown on the wheel, stamped with the maker's name, dipped and fired. Occasionally handles, made by pressing in a mould, were added before the dipping.

The decorated wares, however, called for a more elaborate treat-

---

(1) Cf. *Plate* 4B.

ment, more numerous workmen, and a degree of specialization and subdivision within the factory. The decoration was effected by means of hemispherical bowl-like moulds, in the inside of which the designs had been impressed by means of stamps (1). The first step in the process, therefore, and the most important, was the preparation of the stamps. The dependence of relief-decorated pottery on metal prototypes has already been emphasized, and evidence has accumulated to show that, at least in some cases, castings were made direct from metal vessels, and the potters' stamps prepared from these. An exact correspondence of designs occurring on silver and pottery has hitherto been noted only once, on a silver cup from a grave at Hoby in Denmark, and its pottery copy. It must always be remembered, however, that silver vessels pay in the melting-pot the price of their own intrinsic value; pots survive, if only in fragments. At least one instance is known in which two stamps, otherwise identical, differ in only one slight detail, suggesting that parts of both were taken from one negative mould, and it is readily believable that this might have been a casting from metalwork. Sometimes, however, variations in pattern-units in different moulds (that is, the moulds from which the pots themselves were taken) seem to be due to the combination of different stamps: thus, an identical torso may have different heads, or the attributes held by a figure may change from pot to pot.

With the positive stamp, which in all preserved examples is of clay, was made a negative impression on the interior of the mould. The arrangement of the design, and the selection of the stamps to be used, were possibly the work of a second slave. The mould, having been turned on the wheel, was divided into horizontal zones by means either of plain lines or of simple repetitive patterns, such as the rosette or the egg-and-dart, sometimes made by the use of a 'roulette' (a small wheel having the desired pattern on its outer edge), sometimes by the repetition of a single stamp. Within the zones demarcated in this way, the main pattern-field was divided vertically by the impression of stamps bearing designs of tripods, pillars, trees, etc. In the best period this division was almost invariably by four or multiples of four, a similar strict balance being also observed within the fields so obtained. In these spaces were impressed any decorative details, and finally any figures used. The permutations available to the artist were very numerous, although a skilled man might produce a very satisfactory result by the use of an astonishingly small number of stamps. The last process of all in making the mould was the freehand drawing with the *stilus*, to fill in all the lacunae in the design—grass on the

---

(1) *Plates* 4B *and* 5B.

ground, stems connecting the leaves and flowers in a wreath, or ribbons suspending a mask from its peg. These additions often reveal the idiosyncrasies of a mould-maker whose identity would otherwise lie undetected beneath the impersonality of the stamps he used. Finally, the mould was fired.

In the making of a pot, the mould prepared in the way described was mounted on the potter's wheel, and clay pressed into it and smoothed on the inside by the thrower, who probably also at this stage worked the rim of the vessel above the edge of the mould. The clay was then allowed to dry, and in drying it contracted sufficiently to enable the shell to be detached from the mould. The bowl-shaped shell might then be given greater height by the addition of a short or tall foot (1).

The decoration of Arretine relief-pottery (and of the analogous wares of the Cn. Ateius firm (1)) is of two main types—large figural representations[1] (2) and designs made up of formal decorative elements (3). The figural designs follow different formulae. They may be repetitions, as in the bowls representing four pairs of diners reclining on their couches, or two companies, each of two old and two young satyrs at the wine-treading: or they may reveal an essentially processional design such as the march of the Seasons (4), or a succession of 'Kalathiskos' dancers, all moving in the same direction (5). Occasionally the bowl tells a story from mythology or from the contemporary drama, but this is a relatively rare occurrence.

The grouping of figures in the earliest Arretine wares was kept rigidly disciplined in strict balance, the field of decoration being normally divided on a binary system. In this stern classicism, and in the exquisite quality of the work lavished on its interpretation, lies the great charm of the earliest and best Arretine wares. In the later works the binary system breaks down, sometimes producing nonsensical versions of the carefully composed earlier designs, the quality of the mould-impressions deteriorates, and the free-hand drawing is carelessly and summarily done.

The Arretine wares with conventional designs exploit to the full the repertory of forms which belongs to the minor arts of the Hellenistic and early Imperial periods. Wreaths, masks, scrolls, swags of fruit and flowers are marshalled in neat order between formal borders of dots, rosettes or egg-and-dart, and amongst them flutter little cupids, or birds and butterflies, rendered with a delightful naturalism (6), a

[1] From which is derived the term 'terra sigillata', or 'figured clay', often misleadingly applied to all the red-gloss wares of the Western factories.

(1) Cf. *Plates* 4A and 5A; (2) *Plates* 4A and B; (3) *Plate* 6; (4) *Plate* 4A; (5) *Plate* 4B; (6) *Plate* 5B.

naturalism which finds its perfect expression in a famous bowl at Mainz, on which cranes stoop and strut amidst tall water-plants (1).

The inspiration of Arretine pottery has been sought, and thought to have been found, in many places. The figure-subjects owed much to the revived classicism of the 'neo-Attic' reliefs, and many parallels may be found among the minor arts of all kinds, but it should be borne in mind that these do not necessarily derive one from the other, but are alike because all breathed a common air. On one of these arts, however, Arretine pottery clearly appears to have depended—that of the silver-smith. That Arretine mould-stamps were actually obtained from silver vessels has been shown above, and is clearly suggested by a passage in Pliny. This dependence, however, extends beyond individual borrowings of motifs. The handled cup-forms of Arretine pottery, for instance, may be exactly paralleled in the silver cups of such treasures as that from Boscoreale, now in the Louvre, and their ring-handles are such as would not normally be evolved by the potter. Again, the bowl with cranes referred to above (2) is no more than a successful ceramic copy of an Augustan silver bowl like one which has survived the perils of the intervening centuries and is now in the Morgan Library in New York.

Much has been said here about the decorated forms of Arretine pottery, and it remains to mention those plain wares which, though often relied upon by the archaeologist for dating, otherwise tend to be passed over in silence. Influenced though they too were by the dominance of metal, they achieved a clean and precise beauty of their own which can often only be recreated by an effort of the imagination from a shattered and rubbed thing, only part preserved and indifferently repaired. The most common shapes were flat dishes of various sizes, with sharply profiled rims and feet (3), and cups which, in their slanting sides and in the finish of rim and foot, showed the same metallic qualities (4). These are delightful in their cleanness and crispness, but there were also other forms of cup which, in the curves of their profiles, showed a greater feeling for clay without any loss of sharpness. These cups may be regarded as the first signs of the ultimate emancipation of the potter from the smith. In late Augustan and Tiberian times the plain forms began to be decorated with slight impressed or incised ornamentation, and occasionally with applied relief decoration in the form of little S-shaped handles and other small motives. Numerous moulds for these ornaments have been found, and it is clear that they were used by a considerable number of potters both in Arretium and elsewhere in Northern Italy.

---

(1) *Plate* 5A; (2) *Plate* 5A; (3) *Plate* 8B; (4) *Plate* 8A.

Pliny, in the passage which has already been referred to in connection with Samian ware, writes: 'Renown in this still attaches to Arretium, in Italy, and, for cups only, to Surrentum (the modern Sorrento on the Gulf of Naples), Hasta, Pollentia . . . in Italy too Mutina produces its own wares.' Of the cups of Surrentum nothing is known archaeologically, but two other sites in Southern Italy have produced evidence that pottery was made there in the Arretine manner. One of these, PUTEOLI, was the most important harbour in Italy in early Imperial times, and a considerable pottery industry appears to have been situated there, most of the potters making plain wares, but at least one also producing relief-decorated ware in the style of the Perennius factory. The second centre was CALES, which appears to have continued in production from the second century B.C. and to have adapted itself, however modestly, to the Arretine manner.

Of the North Italian towns mentioned by Pliny, only MUTINA (the modern Modena) has produced archaeological evidence to suggest that its potters made wares resembling the Arretine in general character, and that there was perhaps some even more direct connection with Arretium. The North Italian potteries appear to have done a considerable export trade with the barbarian provinces of Raetia, Noricum, Pannonia and Upper Germany, but their greatest period of prosperity falls somewhat later than that of Arretium, only finally dying away in the reign of Vespasian.

There can be little question, however, but that Arretine pottery claimed the greatest renown in early Imperial times. It found its way to the most distant parts—to Britain on the one hand and to India on the other—and it was able, for instance, to penetrate the markets of such sophisticated and luxurious Hellenistic centres as Antioch. That its prestige stood high is shown by the fact that the stamp 'Genuine Arretine' appears on pottery which is, in fact, not Arretine at all. Its exact status as a tableware, however, is difficult to assess. It ranked well below silver and probably below bronze, and it has been suggested that the rise of the glass industry had something to do with the decline of the pottery industry. Nor do the pottery towns themselves appear to have been wealthy; if the capitalists who owned the factories were indeed rich, they lived away from the sources of their wealth. Be that as it may, Arretine pottery was the noblest of its kind. When it got broken, it was worth riveting, as more than one example shows (1).

It is not easy to specify precisely when the Arretine industry finally declined into complete insignificance. The finds from the German

---

(1) Cf. *Plate* 7A

frontier area suggest that Arretine pottery ceased to be exported there after the first quarter of the first century A.D., but this may mean no more than that Arretine had been driven away from those markets by Gaulish wares. At Camulodunum (Colchester), however, the Gaulish wares are not found in the layers of habitation representing the period before the conquest of Britain (A.D. 44). The poet Martial (who was in Rome from about 64 until 95 A.D.) refers twice to Arretine pottery, on neither occasion in complimentary terms, but one cannot be sure whether by this time the word 'Arretine' had not come to mean no more than 'earthenware', just as 'Samian' had done before. The complimentary notice given by Pliny, on the other hand, seems to be specific in its reference to Arretium. It is ironic that the same eruption of Vesuvius which overwhelmed him in A.D. 79 also buried in an earthenware seller's shop, and thus preserved for posterity, an unpacked case of imported Gaulish pots—the clearest possible indication of the extent to which, by this date, the Gaulish had superseded the Arretine economically, even in Italy itself. Nevertheless, there are indications from sites in Africa that Arretine, or at least Italian, ware was being exported to that province as late as the Antonine period.

Gaul

The cause of the ascendancy of Gaulish pottery is to be sought in the economic facts of the time and perhaps, to a lesser degree, in its own material superiority to Arretine, for it was of a stouter fabric and a superior gloss. Decentralization of industry was a marked feature of the growing Roman Empire, and the pottery industry tended to move nearer both to its best established customers—the Roman legions— and to the newly romanized provinces, with their growing demands for the material things of Roman culture. That the industry in South Gaul was a development of the Italian seems clear from the derivation of some South Gaulish from Italian (particularly Puteolan) shapes, and from the appearance in South Gaul at an early date of potters' names which also occur on Italian wares. It is not unlikely that some of the first establishments in South Gaul were in fact offshoots of factories in Italy. That the potters were mobile enough is shown by their migrations within Gaul itself, and by the finding at Mainz of a mould-fragment of an early type, suggesting that potters had moved to keep up with their legionary market before normal channels of supply had been fully developed to the Rhine and beyond.

Within Gaul itself, moreover, a similar centrifugal process may be seen. The earliest centres, which commenced production early in the reign of Tiberius, are those of South Gaul, in the territory of the Ruteni tribe. The most important were MONTANS, BANASSAC and

B   17

especially LA GRAUFESENQUE, all in the general area of Toulouse. From there a steady north-eastwards movement is observable, first to a group of factories in the territory of the Arverni tribe, in the general vicinity of Vichy, and then to a far more widely dispersed range of centres in the large area lying roughly between the upper reaches of the River Marne and the stretch of the Rhine below Mainz as far as the Swiss frontier. The shift to central Gaul, the chief centre of which was LEZOUX, began in the reign of Claudius, and the onward movement occupied roughly the first half of the second century.

The north-eastward shift and the passage of time coincide with a change in the stylistic character of the Gaulish pottery itself. The early South Gaulish wares observe the forms of Augustan naturalism in art. Their favourite subject-matter is plant life of all kinds, particularly when disciplined into the running scroll of stems and leaves which lies at the very heart of Augustan art and may be seen on such a central manifestation of that art as the great Altar of Peace erected in Rome by Augustus himself. The absence of figural decoration is striking, and proclaims that the South Gaulish potters were almost entirely independent of the influence of Arretium in the composition of their ornaments, if not wholly in their choice of vessel shapes. Yet, despite the subject matter of their decoration, and its obvious dependence on the sources which inspired Augustan art, there is a noticeable tendency in Gaul for natural forms to evolve into simplified stenographs, and for the articulation of organic growth to become disjointed; the leisurely flowing curves are forced into angularities (1), and the forms of living things are constrained to make pure patterns. At first designs were mainly organized in horizontal zones, a scheme to which the plant-scrolls, wreaths, floral arcadings and so forth were admirably suited. This predilection for horizontal patterning was partly imposed by the shape of bowl that was the favourite vessel of this period (2), in which a central cordon separated the almost vertical-sided upper part from the rounded lower part. That this horizontal system had some innate appeal for the Gaulish potter, however, is suggested by the fact that even the later hemispherical bowl (3), the body of which was not formed in this way, was often divided for decorative purposes into superimposed friezes. A further tendency showed itself in the potters' habit, which grew from small beginnings just before the middle of the first century A.D., of dividing his horizontal zones vertically into alternating panels ('metope' decoration), medallions, arcades, and so forth (4).

Parallel with this tendency in point of time, but divergent from it

---

(1) *Plate 7*A; (2) *Plate 7*B; (3) cf. *Plate 12*A; (4) *Plate 7*B.

B. *Bowl, with marbled decoration and stamp of the potter Castus.*
Found at Bordighera. La Graufesenque. Mid-1st century A.D.
Diam. $4\frac{1}{4}$ *in.*
British Museum (*G. & R.*). *See page* 20

in spirit and intention, is the so-called 'free style', in which animal and human forms were freely disposed over a given field of decoration (1). This style was frequently distressingly feeble, not least when ranges of figures were superimposed in horizontal schemes of decoration, where it is essential for clarity that all the components of the design should be ranged on one base-line. Nevertheless, the hunting-scenes frequently chosen as subjects (2), although drawn originally from classical sources, evoked a response in the Celtic artist which enabled him, when freed from the restraints of Greco-Roman culture and the limitations of the moulding technique, to produce the master-pieces of native art discussed below (pp. 34–5). These were indeed often anticipated by red-gloss wares on which the designs had been drawn by means of a 'slip' of creamy consistency freely trailed on in the manner of icing-sugar on a cake (3). The lively style of these slip-decorated ('en barbotine') wares had been preceded by the use, as early as the second half of the first century A.D., of stylized plant and leaf-forms on the rims of dishes (4). These motifs continued in use until at least the third century (5) and were sometimes combined with a decoration of overlapping scales (6), which was itself occasionally used alone with great effect (7). The slip technique could also be combined with the use of decorative motifs pressed in a mould and then luted to the body of the vessel (8), a procedure occasionally employed by itself.

The second century, when the economic lead in the pottery in-dustry had passed to Central Gaul, and to LEZOUX in particular, saw the introduction of the human figure into the potters' decorative repertory, mythological subjects being especially favoured. But the economic success of Lezoux, which was assured of a great export trade thanks to its strategic position at the nexus of an important system of waterways, was accompanied by marked artistic decline. The for-malizing tendencies already described, the excessive sub-division of the decorative field, and the feeble rendering of the human figure, resulted in incoherent designs of little or no artistic worth. This pro-cess of degradation was carried even further in the potteries of the eastern part of the province, where ornamental elements, borrowed from both Southern and Central Gaul, were combined in meaningless patterns over the surface of the vessel. These tendencies towards dis-integration of design and debasement of form were even more marked in the relief-decorated pottery produced in more marginal provinces such as Pannonia, Britain or Spain.

*   *   *   *   *

---

(1) *Plate* 12A; (2) *Plate* 12A; (3) *Frontispiece, Plates* 20 and 21; (4) Cf. *Plate* 24B; (5) *Plate* 19; (6) *Plate* 12B; (7) *Plate* 17; (8) *Frontispiece*.

The temptations which seduced into empty vulgarity the maker of relief-decorated wares did not, however, equally afflict the potter who was content with plain forms and less pretentious modes of decoration.

The Roman artisan frequently attempted to imitate in a base material the outward appearance of a more precious one, as has already been seen in the course of this chapter (p. 13). The glass-maker, in particular, imitated natural semi-precious stones with his factitious material, making clear colourless glass in counterfeit of rock-crystal, and striped and banded glass to look like stones with natural markings. The potter in his turn produced a 'marbled' ware, probably in imitation of the latter type of glass. This pottery had a yellow gloss-coating with markings in red, apparently obtained by removing the yellow layer in places with a brush or feather and exposing the red beneath (1). This was a distinct addition to the potter's repertory, but one which had no lasting influence. Similar effects have been attained in the history of pottery at widely separate times and places, but they have usually been achieved by kneading together clays of different colours (cf. p. 29 below), or by using such a mixture as a surface wash. The Roman potters' contribution is therefore technically unique and deserves due notice. 'Marbled' ware was made in Italy, but its short heyday was enjoyed in the South of Gaul, particularly at La Graufe-senque, and was restricted to approximately the period from the reign of Claudius to that of Vespasian.

A further borrowing of the potter, again from the glass-maker, may be seen in the red-gloss pottery decorated by incisions obviously imitating the facets of cut glass. Ranging from the simplest patterns to representational designs, this form of decoration found its happiest expression in the rendering of star-like forms on the rounded surfaces of flagons (2) and of small globular jugs (3). This technique was practised mainly at Lezoux and at some of the East Gaulish potteries, from the second century onwards.

Akin in method to this form of decoration, but less striking in its results, was the use of rouletting. This specifically ceramic technique begins to be used alone for decorating red-gloss pottery in the second and third centuries A.D. It had continued in practice as an ancillary of moulded decoration on Arretine ware, and as a mode of ornament in its own right on coarse pottery, through the first century. Its emergence on red-gloss pottery must be regarded as a symptom of the decline in prestige of relief-moulding, and the re-assertion of the wheel's part in pottery-making (4). That the thrower's art was never lost, despite the

(1) *Colour Plate* B; *Plate* 10B; (2) *Plate* 14; (3) *Plate* 15; (4) *Plate* 13A.

seductions of the moulding-processes, is amply demonstrated by the range of splendid plain forms, clean and crisp, which constitute artistically perhaps the outstanding achievement of Roman red-gloss pottery (1). W. B. Honey, in *The Potter's Art*, justly relates these terse and simple shapes to the practical engineering temper revealed in those aqueducts and roads which are the most lasting monuments of the creative genius of Rome.

Late Roman Wares

Just as Italian pottery had been copied in Gaul and eventually superseded, so the Gaulish red-gloss pottery was in its turn copied in other provinces of the Empire. Thus the Gaulish bowl-shape illustrated on Plate 7B, which can be dated to the late first century A.D., was copied (2) in a ware ('LATE B' WARE) with a surface apparently produced by burnishing an orange-red wash, rather than by the process described earlier in this chapter (pp. 5–6). On some examples, a continuous spiral from the centre betrays the method by which this was done on the wheel (3). The commonest shapes were dishes (4), sometimes with a broad flat rim, and deep and shallow bowls (5). The decoration of this ware, at first restricted to simple grooves or rouletted bands, with the passage of time became elaborated by the use of a growing repertory of stamped devices. The earliest were of palm-like leaves radially placed, and of concentric circles and small trellis-motives, often enclosed within a rouletted herring-bone band; to these purely formal motives were added friezes of animals, human heads, and finally Christian symbols. The earliest specimens of this pottery appear to date from the second century, and it is likely that it began to be made contemporaneously with, or shortly after, the Gaulish bowls referred to above. It continued to be made at least until the sixth century. It was exported all over the Eastern Mediterranean, but the abundance of fragments and whole pots found in North Africa, and the presence there of the earliest shapes, make it likely that the centre of its manufacture was situated there. It has been plausibly suggested that during the second century—a period of great prosperity for the Roman East—the use of pottery waned in favour of metal and glass, and that local manufacture declined or perished: with the onset of harder times in the third century, the demand for pottery grew and had to be met from abroad. An apparent scarcity of this pottery on Eastern Mediterranean sites during the fifth century may well be explained, on the hypothesis of an African origin, by the fact

(1) *Plates* 9B, 10A, 11A and B, 26; (2) *Plate* 24A; (3) *Plate* 22B; (4) *Plate* 23B; Cf., however, *Plate* 23A; (5) *Plate* 24A and B.

that the Vandals overran North Africa in about 430 and occupied it until early in the sixth century. This red burnished ware with stamped decoration was occasionally copied by local potters in the towns to which it was exported.

Closely akin to this pottery, and in some cases so similar that the two cannot be distinguished with assurance, is a ware ('LATE A' WARE) made of a fine red clay, thin and fired hard, with a thin red surface-wash. This varies from glossy to matt, and it seems more likely that the surface, when glossy, has been burnished, rather than produced by the technique employed for Arretine and Gaulish pottery. The shapes favoured were shallow bowls and flat dishes (1), often of considerable diameter, and were based on contemporary metal forms. The rims of the bowls were sometimes decorated with figures of animals or fish moulded in relief, but otherwise the ornamentation was restricted to a band of rouletting, often of a fine sharp quality, round the rim (2) or centre of the well. This ware is found on sites throughout the Eastern Mediterranean, in Syria, Palestine, Cyprus and Egypt, but also occasionally in the West, on the Adriatic coast and in Spain. By far the largest quantities, however, are found in North Africa, and it is probable that it was made either there or in Egypt. Its presence at Dura-Europos (2) in Syria (sacked in A.D. 256) indicates that it was being made at least by the middle of the third century A.D., and the apparent suddenness of its emergence on Syrian sites and elsewhere would suggest that it may have been in production and distributed in its own locality even earlier. It seems to have ceased either being manufactured or being exported not later than the first quarter of the fifth century A.D.

Apparently made of the same clay is a series of relief-decorated fragments belonging to rectangular trays with flat rim and sunken centre, and flat sloping sides connecting them. These are frequently decorated with heads and motives in circular frames obviously adapted from medallions, but sometimes also with figural compositions. Comparisons with coin-types and with silver plate, from which these trays were obviously copied, suggest a date in the fourth or possibly the early fifth century. The fragments hitherto known all come from Egypt, and tend to strengthen the claim of an Egyptian origin for this whole class.

The place of this pottery, on its disappearance early in the fifth century, was taken by yet another red ware ('LATE C' WARE) with impressed decoration. Like the other local red fabrics which imitated the true red-gloss pottery, its physical characteristics varied. Normally,

---

(1) *Plate* 25A; (2) *Plate* 13B.

however, it was potted thin and fired hard, and the surface tended rather to be a matt red wash than a gloss. As with the pottery of the preceding two groups, its favourite shapes were the bowl and the dish, and these were ornamented with leaf-motives or animal figures impressed in outline within a circular rouletted frame. Christian emblems, such as the jewelled cross frequently appear. Like the previous imitation red-gloss wares described, it is very widely distributed throughout the Eastern Mediterranean, and may possibly have been made in Egypt. Its manufacture appears to have gone on well into Islamic times and so passes outside the scope of this book.

*   *   *   *   *

The 'red-gloss' wares treated in this chapter are by no means completely homogeneous. The surface-quality which they all have in common varies considerably in brilliance of sheen and intensity of colour, and may not in all examples even have been produced by exactly the same methods. Nor is it always easy to draw a hard-and-fast line where 'red-gloss' pottery ends and 'coarse' pottery begins, and many writers would extend the meaning of 'terra sigillata' to embrace such diverse types of ware as shiny black pottery on the one hand and 'Nabataean' pottery on the other (see Chap. 3). The admirable jar on Plate 16 is a case in point. It has a slight sheen and a brownish colour, and clearly aspired to be a 'red-gloss' pot. Yet in its surface-qualities it falls far short of the contemporary Gaulish 'terra sigillata' wares, whilst by its form and decoration it is related to the wares dealt with in Chap. 3. The same may be said of the beaker with incised decoration illustrated on Plate 22A.

The uncertainty as to the grouping of these wares is sometimes paralleled, particularly as regards the Near Eastern fabrics, by uncertainty as to where they were made. The 'Pergamene', 'Samian' and other groups outlined in this chapter may prove, as knowledge accumulates, to be less homogeneous and exclusive than at first appeared. Numbers of pots have been recovered in the more easterly parts of the Roman Empire which can only with difficulty be fitted into existing categories (1). Yet they display the essential characteristics of the wares forming the subject-matter of this chapter. The likelihood is that numerous pottery-centres existed in the Aegean lands and further east, all making wares of similar character. This general resemblance supplies the criterion for ranging them with Italian and Gaulish pottery in the great family of Roman 'red-gloss' wares.

(1) cf. Plate 18.

3

GLAZED POTTERY

It is often assumed that glazed wares, in the sense familiar to modern people, were virtually unknown to the Greeks and Romans. This assumption is far from the truth, even if it must be conceded that the brilliant colours and lustrous surface of glazed pottery were more familiar to the eastern Hellenized provincials of the Roman world than to Greeks or Italians.

Lead-glazed Wares

One of the most widespread methods of glazing in the relatively primitive phases of the potter's art has always been the use of lead-compounds. These enjoy the advantages of fusing at relatively low temperatures, of being usable with most types of potter's clay, and of being easily stained with metallic oxides—particularly with copper, which produces a rich green colour.

The origins of lead-glaze are not known, but have sometimes been attributed to Egypt, that mother of inventions in the arts of fire. Whatever its origin, the technique appears to have been first used on a large scale in the Near East during the first century B.C. There exists a fairly large homogeneous class of coloured lead-glazed pottery with relief-decoration produced in a mould after the manner of Arretine ware (see pp. 13–14); within this class a low cup with two ring-handles is by far the most frequently found shape (1). Fragments of moulds for such cups have been found at TARSUS, together with other signs of manufacture there, and there are also indications that they were made at NOTION near Ephesus, and at the known pottery-site of TSCHANDARLI (see p. 9) near Pergamum, all in Asia Minor. These wares were made of well-worked buff clay, which was apparently fired to a 'biscuit' condition before the addition of glaze. In the second firing the cups were placed, sometimes upside down and sometimes the right way up, on saucers which kept them separate and caught any drips of the fluid glaze. These refinements of manufacture probably proved expensive, and the lead-glazed wares had no such universal currency as the red-

(1) *Plate* 28A and *Colour Plate* C.

C. *Cup (scyphus), lead-glazed earthenware. Asia Minor.*
1st century B.C. *or* A.D. *Diam.* $3\frac{1}{4}$ *in.*
British Museum. (G. & R). See page 24

gloss pottery already described. Like that pottery, however, they aimed to imitate metalwork. The moulded decoration is frequently closely paralleled by the *repoussé* work on known silver cups, while the handles, by their shape, clearly betray their derivation. Although these cups predominate, other forms were also made, notably handled jars (1), vases, footed bowls (2), inkwells (3), handleless cups, and small jugs ('askos') copied direct from metalwork (4). The majority of these vessels are decorated with wreaths of leaves and flowers, or with scale-patterns, but figure subjects also occur. One notable cup combines with the figures of Greek warriors an unmistakable Parthian horseman, turning in flight and unloosing on his pursuer that 'Parthian shot' which the Romans had learned to dread at the battle of Carrhae (53 B.C.) and which is so frequently referred to in Latin literature of the Augustan age. The presentation of this theme is, therefore, fully consistent with a date in the first century B.C., while finds at Tarsus indicate that wares of this sort were being made at least into the first century A.D. Most of these pots, when of open form, are coloured green on the outside and yellowish-brown on the inside.

Simple moulded designs were not the only resort of the potter for his decorative effects. Instances are known of designs drawn with great verve and skill by the use of a clay 'slip' of creamy consistency. This is a technique demanding the utmost sureness of touch and admitting of no hesitations or afterthoughts (5). Occasionally also the chromatic range of this pottery was extended. A white slip was used to coat certain portions of the design, with a resultant lightening of the tone of the green glaze; or coloured slips or paints (no doubt with a clay base) were used in polychrome designs which were fixed in the first firing (6). Where ornament of this kind was used, the yellow glaze sometimes replaced the green on the outside of the vessel.

Most of the green- and yellow-glazed wares have been found on the mainland and islands of the Eastern Mediterranean, a distribution which agrees well with their manufacture at the sites mentioned above, and also possibly elsewhere in Asia Minor and North Syria. A number, however, have been found in SOUTH RUSSIA, and the distinct character of some of them suggests that a local manufacture of lead-glazed, as of other, pottery sprang up there as an extension of the industry of Asia Minor. Here there appears to have been a predilection in design for grotesque and satirical subjects (7), and in technique for the barbotine drawing, combined with the use of underglaze slip, mentioned in the preceding paragraph.

---

(1) *Plate* 27; (2) cf. *Plate* 4A; (3) *Plate* 29A; (4) cf. *Plate* 31B; (5) *Plates* 29B and 30A; (6) *Plate* 31A; (7) *Plates* 30A and 31A.

Lead-glazing seems to have spread early to ITALY, but the exact nature of the pottery made there is not yet fully understood, although the new glaze was certainly used on lamps (1) and figurines, and probably also on cups, vases and other vessels (2) with relief-decoration. By the middle of the first century A.D. the use of lead-glaze had reached the Allier district of France, where ST. RÉMY-EN-ROLLAT, VICHY and GANNAT appear to have been the main centres of manufacture of wares with a greenish-yellow or brownish glaze on a light-coloured body. The vessels made were chiefly cups and a type of handled jug ornamented on its upper part with curious arcaded patterns (3). These were produced in a mould from which the whole of the upper part of the body of the vessel was taken, as if it had been a bowl inverted. Small flasks in the form of animals, often very charmingly rendered, were also made (4). The pottery town of LEZOUX too appears, at a later date, to have made wares of a fine white clay covered with a green glaze. Pottery of this class is often decorated with motifs, sometimes hunting-scenes, drawn in 'slip', and these characteristics, taken in conjunction with the circumstances under which some of the pieces were found, suggest that they were made as late as the third century. Since, however, green- and yellow-glazed wares were certainly made in COLOGNE from about A.D. 200, and probably also in BONN, it is likely that many of the pieces found in the Rhineland were also made there (5).

A kiln of the second century A.D. which made green-glazed wares of the type under discussion has been excavated at HOLT, in Denbighshire. The methods used—of firing pieces upside-down, supported on stilts enclosed within bowl-shaped 'saggers'—are reminiscent of those used at Tarsus, and some connexion with Oriental practice may be suspected. Some at least of the green-glazed pottery found in Britain (6) was therefore probably of indigenous origin, although some was also undoubtedly imported from the Continent. This is the case with another type of lead-glazed pottery, which, long ignored as being post-medieval in date, has now been shown to be definitely of late first or early second century date. This pottery has a coarse red body and often thick brown glaze, and was probably made in Northern Gaul or the Rhineland. Green-glazed pottery, of coarse quality and often barbaric form, was also made in the Central European province of PANNONIA (7).

---

(1) *Plate* 30B; (2) *Plate* 31B; (3) *Plate* 32; (4) *Plate* 33A and B; (5) *Plates* 34, 36–7, 38A, 39A; (6) *Plate* 38B; (7) *Plate* 35.

GLAZED POTTERY

Glazed Quartz Frit Ware

A method of producing a brilliant blue glaze was known in EGYPT at a very early date. It was probably first discovered accidentally by observing the action in a fire of natron (a substance found in a natural state in Egypt) on a quartz stone coated with the malachite used by the ancient Egyptians as an eye-paint. Quartz-stone being a difficult substance to shape, substitutes for it were probably found in the form of the softer stone, steatite, or of powdered quartz; the one being shaped by cutting, the other by moulding. This powdered quartz ware is usually known as 'faïence', but since that word is properly reserved for the tin-glazed earthenwares such as *maiolica* or 'delftware', it should perhaps more properly be called 'glazed quartz frit ware'. The quartz stones could be glazed merely by the action of natron or certain plant-ashes used as a flux, in combination with malachite or other copper compounds acting as colouring media; but this mixture has been found by experiment to be inadequate for producing a glaze on a body of powdered quartz. If, however, a glaze produced in this way is itself pulverized and used to coat the powdered quartz body, a satisfactory glaze results, and this was no doubt the method used in Ancient Egypt, as it also is by the modern forgers of antiquities in that country.

A great disadvantage of this type of ware lies in the difficulty of shaping the friable quartz body. It has been found, however, that by the addition of a solution of natron and water the mass becomes plastic enough to be shaped in a mould or roughly fashioned with the fingers. An even greater plasticity can be got by adding salt and water to the quartz powder. Since both natron and salt are changed in the firing to the same compound, sodium silicate, and cannot therefore be distinguished by analysis, there is no way of deciding positively which means the Egyptian potter used; but since some at least of the later wares appear to have been turned on the wheel, the method favouring the greatest plasticity seems to suggest itself.

In the course of time the potter of dynastic Egypt extended his colour-range to embrace black, red, apple-green, purple, yellow and white. Nor was he content with plain coloured wares. At least as early as the XII Dynasty (twentieth century B.C.) a most effective painting was being done in black pigment on the lustrous turquoise-blue glaze, a technique later exploited with brilliant effect by the potters of the Islamic Near East. In the interim, however, this technique appears to have languished, if not altogether to have died out. Its place during the Hellenistic period was taken by a method of producing designs in low relief and colouring them to contrast with the ground on which they stand. By this means wares of exquisite quality, usually in delicate pale colouring and with a rather matt surface, were produced (1). During the same period were made wine-jugs with applied relief-decoration in the form of royal portraits of the reigning dynasty of the Ptolemies.

In the Roman period the glaze of the quartz frit ware tends to be stronger in tone and glassier in appearance than formerly, possibly in response to the contemporary taste for coloured glass. The vase shown on Coloured Plate D reflects this appeal not only in its brilliant turquoise glaze, but in its very shape and the details of its handle-terminals. That the more delicate tones of the wares with colour-contrasts could still be produced at will, however, is well shown by the fact that plates of this sort were found as kiln-wasters on a pottery site at MEMPHIS; the interior of each bears a design in subdued tones of green and purple, while the back is coloured a rich brilliant turquoise. These plates were found in company with other plates, bowls and trays, which were clearly of Roman date, and which were covered solely with the richer glaze. Whereas in the Hellenistic era the maker of these wares had prevented his colours from running by producing his designs in distinct relief, the potters of the Roman period had sufficient control of their medium to achieve the same results merely by surface washes, with a consequently greater freedom and a more linear character in the rendering of their designs (2).

Relief-wares, however, did not cease with the advent of the Roman era. The two Hellenistic traditions of monochrome pottery with applied moulded relief on the one hand, and of polychrome pottery with low relief on the other, appear to merge in the Roman period. This fusion of styles is represented by wares decorated in high relief, apparently by carving (3), and brilliantly coloured in various tones of turquoise, blue and green. It is not impossible, however, that this technique may trace unbroken descent to dynastic times, when objects both of glazed steatite and of glazed quartz frit were ornamented by carving, and occasionally even by piercing, to produce a design à jour. Little is known of the dating of the glazed quartz frit ware in the Roman period, but that carved work of the kind described was practised at least as early as the first century A.D. is proved by the discovery at Pompeii (destroyed A.D. 79) of a cylindrical cup and a stand decorated with animals and fish in a frieze below a running wave-border. A fragment of a vase of the same shape has been found at Tarsus in Asia Minor in a context also suggesting a date in the first century A.D. Akin to this carving technique was the method of incis-

---

(1) *Plate* 39B; (2) *Plate* 42A; (3) *Plate* 43A.

D. *Amphora, glazed quartz frit ware. Egypt.*
Probably 1st century A.D. *Ht.* $10\frac{3}{5}$ *in.*
Kelekian Collection. See page 28

ing a pattern in the body of a monochrome piece, with the result that, since the glaze ran thicker in the incisions, the design appeared in a deeper tone than that of the ground colour (1).

Further technical resources were at the disposal of the Roman-Egyptian maker of glazed quartz frit ware. A form of relief-decoration could be obtained by applying shreds of body material, usually to suggest laurel-wreaths coloured green on a dark blue or purple ground (2). Fragments of one or more of these vessels have been found at Dura-Europos, in Syria, and must therefore date before the mid-third century A.D. A rarer technique was the kneading together of dark and light bodies to produce a marbled effect below the transparent glaze (cf. p. 20 above).

The workers of dynastic times had made innumerable figures from the glazed quartz frit material, and literally thousands of clay-moulds used for this purpose have been found in Egypt. There were also, however, more ambitious attempts at modelling, and the British Museum possesses a remarkable realistic portrait-head of one of the queens of the Ptolemies. Both traditions continue into the Roman period. On the one hand are figures, probably mass-produced, representing Greek subjects, such as Venus Anadyomene, or archaising Egyptian subjects, such as the god Bes. The portrait tradition, however, also survived in fine heads of Augustus and Tiberius (3) and seems to have continued until as late as the fifth century A.D. Decorations virtually modelled in the round were also used on vessels, no doubt with splendid effect (4).

The prime disadvantage of the glazed quartz frit ware—its lack of plasticity—probably ensured that it did not survive as a potter's material. The splendid colours of its alkaline glaze, however, can hardly be surpassed, and in the Islamic period the Egyptian potter re-emerged with a ware which combined this surface splendour of colour with a substance capable of embodying the virtues of wheel-turning. This was achieved by the use of a clay which contained a high percentage of silica (sand, powdered quartz or the like), for without this an alkaline glaze cannot adhere to its body. The secret of this technique, however, had in fact been known in the Near East hundreds, if not thousands, of years before.

Alkaline-glazed Wares

In the western provinces of the kingdom of Parthia, which marched with the Roman Empire on its eastern frontier and was its great eastern rival, alkaline-glazed pottery was made in considerable quan-

(1) *Plate* 40; (2) *Plate* 41; (3) *Plate* 42B; (4) *Plate* 43B.

tity and (to judge by the different character of pots found in different places) at a number of centres. Traces of manufacture have been found at DURA-EUROPOS on the Euphrates; and the use of glazed coffins, which could hardly be transportable objects of trade, at centres further south, such as SELEUCIA and WARKA (Uruk) on the Tigris, and NIPPUR, suggests that these places, too, had their own kilns.

This pottery varies considerably in its physical characteristics, but in general it is made of sandy clay covered with an alkaline glaze which is coloured to various tones of green and blue by the use of iron and copper oxides (the former perhaps unintentionally). Occasionally manganese is found as a colouring-agent, and at Dura-Europos a certain amount of lead oxide is sometimes found in the glaze, possibly to assist in fluxing it; while at Seleucia a few analysed specimens contained tin oxide, which acts as an opacifier, and produced in one instance an opaque green, and in another a milky white glaze. These, however, are exceptional. The pots were thrown on the wheel, or in exceptional instances formed in two sections, which were then joined. They were subjected twice to the kiln—a 'biscuit' and a glaze firing. Very often, especially after the commencement of the Christian era, they were roughly fashioned and carelessly glazed.

The pots made, mainly bowls and vases (1), were decorated, if at all, by the most elementary means. Simple patterns of parallel lines were incised below the glaze (2), or little rivet-like bosses were applied on the shoulder or handle of a vessel (3), thereby perhaps betraying its origins in metalwork. Occasionally the handled jars bear circular or oval applied pads with impressed designs, often of a Hellenistic character (4). This fact, and an occasional reminiscence of form (as between, for instance, the two-handled jar and the Greek amphora), have led scholars to over-emphasize the indebtedness of this pottery to the West. The independent character of Parthian institutions and of Parthian art have been amply demonstrated, however, and it is probable that, although pottery of the type described is found in pre-Parthian Hellenistic levels in Mesopotamia (from about the middle of the second century B.C.), its main appeal was to Asiatics and not to Greeks. It is easier to see it as a pottery continuing a Mesopotamian tradition slightly modified by Hellenism, than as a classical ware progressively becoming more barbaric with the withdrawal of Western influence. Its feelings for form marks it out from any of the glazed wares hitherto treated in the present chapter. Indeed, it is different in character from any other pottery discussed in this book. Many examples of it, however, appear to come from Syria (and at least two

---

(1) *Plates* 44–7; (2) *Plates* 45–6; (3) *Plate* 44; (4) *Plate* 44.

from Egypt), so that, even disregarding the two Roman occupations of Mesopotamia in the second century A.D., there must have been many Roman citizens to whom this colourful pottery was a familiar sight in the service of their homes.

Just as the art of lead-glazing seems to have been diffused from the Near East gradually westwards, so too the technique of using an alkaline glaze may have spread to the western provinces of the Empire. A kiln-site has been discovered at BAVAY, in north-eastern Gaul, at which alkaline-glazing was practised in the third century A.D. This, however, is probably to be regarded as an isolated occurrence.

'COARSE' POTTERY

To attempt a description of all the miscellaneous kinds of pottery used in the households of the Roman Empire would be as difficult as to do the same for the British Empire—for similar reasons of geography and unequal development. Rome extended her political dominion equally over countries of greater and of less civilization than she enjoyed herself. In general, she borrowed from those whose material culture was more advanced than her own, and by her wealth and power attracted to her own service many of their best artists and craftsmen; whilst, on those less civilized, she imposed the Greco-Roman culture so formed, partly through deliberate policy and partly by the natural process which ensures that the poorer emulates the richer. Time, however, is equipped with subtle compensations, and just as it is true that the relatively barbaric craftsman could not fully assimilate Greco-Roman modes of art, so is it equally true that his own concepts of form and rhythm were not wholly subdued by the incursion of a materially superior civilization. The savage hits back; and as the political power of Rome ceased to expand, faltered, and finally receded, so did native provincial ways of life and thought reassert themselves—in the sphere of art not least when, in a disintegrating centralized economy, former channels of supply were cut and the provinces thrown on their own resources. Nothing, however, is without its due effects. If the romanization of native art is (although sad) an interesting process to observe, the ultimate emergence of a subtly modulated provincial idiom is no less so. Both processes are germane to the study of Roman art, pottery not excepted.

Since it is the aim of this book to present Roman pottery as a manifestation of the potter's art and not as a prop to chronology, no attempt is called for (nor would it be possible within the limits imposed by space and the unequal publication of material from different parts of the world) to make a complete survey of the field. The basic excellence of pottery being satisfying form, and it being impossible to treat of this at large, the potter's resources of decorative treatment necessarily present themselves as the main subject-matter of this chapter. This presentation, moreover, perhaps by some inherent logic, accords well with the line of thought sketched in the previous paragraph. Glaze and gloss are surface-treatments. Physically, being clean and watertight, they represent the superior amenity of an advanced civilization. In their cultural aspect, with their oblique references to precious metal, precious stones, and the glass which imitated precious stones, they represent the values of a society superior in wealth. Such wares would tend to be of humble status where the original materials were in use, but in more outlandish parts they would rank as symbols of a higher civilization, while pottery of untreated surface would serve for chores. This pottery would be made locally, and embody a local spirit. Some of it would ape the admired 'civilized' wares and be (like the red-gloss pottery of the Colchester kilns) a Caliban of ceramic history; but much of it was original, and drew on the authentic sources of the potter's art. What it lost in contemporary prestige it gains in the favourable verdict of posterity. A study of Roman 'coarse' pottery, in so far as it is of ceramic interest, therefore, is virtually a study of provincial wares.

A clear case of the survival of pre-Roman feeling is provided by the so-called 'GALLO-BELGIC' wares, which although certainly manufactured in the province of Gallia Belgica and exported from there to such neighbouring areas as Britain, were also made in many other districts in the Northern provinces, as, for instance, at Trier and Heddernheim, at Carden and Cobern in the Rhineland, and possibly in Britain itself (see below). The most characteristic type of this ware has a dark-grey or black, more or less lustrous, surface, as to the character of which some doubt exists, but which was probably produced by firing in a reducing atmosphere.

The makers of this 'Gallo-Belgic' black ware ('terra nigra') seem to have been concerned to emulate Arretine pottery, but there are analogous black wares which are of greater originality and interest. Large numbers of pots with the black surface-gloss generally characteristic of this pottery have been found in the region of Upchurch, Kent (1). It has accordingly been dubbed by former antiquaries 'UPCHURCH WARE', but this term has now been abandoned since there is no positive evidence that pottery was actually made there, and it is more probable that the wares found in the vicinity were imported. Wherever made, these and analogous black and grey pots are often distinguished both in form and decoration. Some of them have a crisp metallic quality of profile (2), with an air of archaic classicism, which is missing from the shapes of much of the pottery more central to the

---

(1) *Plate* 87 ; (2) *Plate* 48.

Roman tradition: nor is this perhaps a mere coincidence, for Celtic pottery had been directly influenced by Greece as early as the fifth century B.C. A most effective form of linear decoration, probably obtained by burnishing before the pot was fired, is sometimes found alone (1), sometimes in combination with incised decoration. Other modes of decoration were rouletting (2) and incisions by means of a comb, sometimes in repeated stabbed patterns resembling rouletting, and, rarely, in linear designs (3). Rows of raised dots were also applied to produce effective geometric designs (4).

Applied clay decoration, also of a formal character, was used on pottery of quite different fabrics from various parts of Europe (5). Some of these, by the use of surface-washes, appear to be imitating red-gloss pottery (6). The effective use of applied clay techniques of this kind was by no means confined to the northern provinces of the Empire (7).

Yet another form of surface treatment, apparently almost exclusively British, may be seen in a family of small jars which began to be made in the north of this country some time after the middle of the first century A.D. In these the surface, whilst still wet, was pulled up by the finger-tips into irregular points (8) or shaped into rough repetitive designs (9). Although probably inspired by early first-century continental imported wares with applied blobs or ridges of clay, the character of these so-called 'RUSTIC' pots is utterly different. They have a spontaneous quality which (their precise shapes apart) should appeal to those who admire the immediacy of effect and the personal touch of some Japanese pottery.

Probably the most effective, however, of all the wares decorated by applied clay techniques is the Northern pottery ornamented by means of trailed 'slip' (cf. p. 19). In Britain a pottery industry, favoured by the presence of excellent local clay and stimulated by the commercial opportunities opened up by the building of Ermine Street as a link between the economic and political capitals of London and York, developed rapidly in the neighbourhood of the modern CASTOR, near Peterborough, in Northamptonshire. Beginning probably in the second century A.D., and flourishing in the third century, it lasted until late in the fourth or early in the fifth century. The slip-decorated ('barbotine') ware of the Castor district was a light-bodied earthenware of varying hardness, with a surface wash which, when fired in a reducing atmosphere, produced a dark surface sometimes modified by tones of purple or red. Its body-material was somewhat coarser than that of the

---

(1) *Plates* 48, 50 and 51; (2) *Plate* 53; (3) *Plate* 52; (4) *Plate* 49; (5) *Plates* 54, 55 and 57; (6) *Plate* 55; (7) *Plate* 56; (8) *Plate* 59; (9) *Plate* 58.

similar pottery made in the RHINELAND, from which district the Castor potters probably originally came. The frequent occurrence of a glossy surface suggests that these wares were treated somewhat like the red-gloss pottery (pp. 5–6), with the difference that they were fired in a reducing atmosphere. A somewhat similar ware was also probably made in GAUL (1).

By far the commonest shape in this ware was that of the footed cup (2). The slip-decoration, which was trailed on the pot before it was dipped, takes the form either of scrolled ornament (3) or of figure and animal subjects, usually in zones demarcated by lines of rouletted dots. Both types of decoration disclose the spirit of pre-Roman 'Celtic' art modified by Roman influences. The scrolled forms (4) may be compared with those of Celtic metalwork, and the rendering of animals in the figural themes is vividly reminiscent of, for instance, the Witham shield in the British Museum. It is curious, and perhaps significant, that in rendering gladiatorial and circus subjects (5), possibly because they were Romanized features of Romano-British life with which he was unfamiliar, the potter seems hampered and ill at ease, whereas in the hunting-scenes the figures come urgently to life and press with vivid movement round the perimeter of the pot (6). The indebtedness of these wares to the Gaulish barbotine-decorated red-gloss pots can be easily detected, both in their subjects and by the presence on both of the ivy-leaf motive (7), but the Castor potter seems to revel in the emancipation from moulded decoration which the Gaulish potter had only tentatively begun. A physically somewhat similar dark-coated pottery, made during the fourth century in the ARGONNE region of what is now France, was effectively decorated by means of rouletting (8) and leaf-shaped incisions which are reminiscent of the 'cut-glass' technique employed in the decoration of red-gloss pottery (9) (see p. 20 above).

The Castor potters were not wholly dependent for their effects on more or less representational designs carried out in barbotine. Not only did they employ shapes admirable in themselves, such as the 'folded' beaker with thumb-indents (10), but they made good use of pure clay-techniques (11) to produce abstract decorative effects. Yet another class of Castor ware consisted of dark glossy pottery with designs in white pipe-clay applied over the surface-wash. The representations of more or less formalized vine-scrolls (12) or the purely abstract patterns

---

(1) *Plate* 60; (2) *Plates* 60 to 63, etc.; (3) *Plates* 60, 61; (4) *Plate* 61; (5) *Plate* 65; (6) *Plates* 62, 63, 64; (7) *Plates* 64, 66A; cf. *Pl*. 19; (8) *Plate* 67B; (9) *Plates* 66B and 67A; (10) *cf. Plate* 68; (11) *Plate* 69; (12) *Plates* 70, 72.

formed of circular blobs and dots and wavy lines, often combined with convivial mottoes (1), are to be found on closely similar wares made in the Rhineland (2).

A second family of white-painted dark pottery is represented amongst the wares produced by kilns in the NEW FOREST area, where, besides much rough pottery for common use, were made plain dark wares of distinguished form (3) and, in the fourth century, bowls with cream-coloured body, a matt red surface wash, and impressed designs of grouped rosettes, stars, crescents, etc. The painted pottery, however, differs markedly from the Castor and German wares, not only in its shapes, but in the character of its decoration, which consists exclusively of abstract designs built up of straight lines (4) and circles, appearing sometimes almost like the diagrams accompanying a geometrical demonstration. The heyday of this pottery fell in the late third and the fourth centuries A.D.

Effective painted pottery of types other than those already mentioned was also produced in Britain (5).

In the RHINELAND, apart from the white-'painted' dark pottery just mentioned, a strikingly effective type of abstract painting was practised at a pottery in or near SPEICHER-IN-DER-EIFEL (6). The decorated jugs made there date from the late third and fourth centuries. An analogous but more mechanical style of decoration may be seen in a class of wares with marbled decoration, apparently made at a centre in CARDEN-AN-DER-MOSEL. The marbling seems to have been effected by sponging or brushing a brown-burning surface-wash on a darker red-brown body. The forms made, while consisting mainly of one- and two-handled jugs with rounded bodies of shapes familiar in other wares, also included a distinctive type of two-handled bowl and a tapering cylindrical jug with strap-handle which looks forward to the pottery of medieval times. This pottery was occasionally crudely overpainted with designs in white, a fourth-century characteristic, and even the earlier, and technically finer, examples can scarcely be dated much before the beginning of the third century.

Painted pottery of great beauty was made in NUBIA. This country, although never conquered by Rome, suffered the occupation of the northern territory which formed its boundary with Egypt (23 B.C.) and came under some form of Roman suzerainty. In the peace which followed, there was considerable prosperity in Lower Nubia, and the abundant pottery made there in this period reveals strong Roman influence, as may be seen from a comparison of Plate 78 with Plates 18

---

(1) *Plate 72*; (2) *Plates 71, 73*; (3) *Plate 68*; (4) *Plates 74, 75*; (5) *Plates 77, 82B*; (6) *Plate 76*.

or 83A, or of the 'hanging lip' of Plate 79 with that of Plate 9A. These painted wares reveal an adaptation of Greco-Roman formulae in which classical correctness gives way before the urgency of a bold and rhythmic brushwork (1) or the compulsion of an indigenous feeling for form (2). Nor was the pot-painter limited to merely abstract designs, but was capable of a superbly taut and vital stylization of natural form, as in the rendering of the dog on Plate 80, where faithful observation yields nothing to the temptation to caricature always present when a shape in nature is reduced to a formula. In his rendering of the human figure the artist has turned his back on the intervening centuries of Hellenism, and returned to the conventions of Ancient Egypt, combining profile head with the frontal body, and stylizing the features of the face in a way which gives it, with the emphatic eye and enigmatic ear, a mysterious compelling force. Here, too, the barbarian, having assimilated, however imperfectly, the conventions of Greco-Roman art, has gone beyond them.

Similar qualities of formalized design may be observed in the pinkish-buff pottery, usually painted in black pigments on a red ground, of the Christian period in EGYPT, although no positive connection with the earlier wares appears to be traceable (3).

A transmutation of Hellenism similar to that of the Nubian pottery is seen in the 'NABATAEAN' painted wares found in *South Palestine* and *Trans-Jordan*, in territory roughly coterminous with the sphere of influence of the ancient Arab caravan-city of *Petra*. This settlement, dominating the trade-routes leading overland from Arabia and Egypt, grew in wealth and power during the Hellenistic period. The highest point of the city's prosperity and influence, however, was reached under the early Roman Empire, until it was humbled by the Emperor Trajan in A.D. 106 and incorporated in the province of Arabia. The pottery of Roman date found within the area of this Nabataean kingdom varies considerably in physical characteristics. Usually brick-red, tending to a pinkish tone, it is sometimes, in coarser specimens, brownish in colour. Some of the unpainted pieces, being decorated with rouletting, are obviously influenced by the red-gloss pottery, and have been classed as a provincial variant of 'terra sigillata'. Of the painted wares, however, although some are relatively coarse, others are made from finely levigated clay and potted to an almost 'egg-shell' thinness, and analogies have been observed between these wares and the similarly thinly-fashioned pottery of Parthian Mesopotamia. This latter pottery, however, is normally plain, while the especial merit of the Nabataean lies in its painting. Executed for the most part on the

(1) *Plates* 78, 79; (2) *Plate* 80; (3) *Plate* 81.

insides of the bowls and dishes, this painting was carried out by means of a wash, presumably iron-bearing, which burned to a darkish red, sometimes tending to a brownish or mauve tone. There were several different styles of painting, although it cannot be said with certainty whether these differences are due to place (as is most likely), or to time. The most effective of them, unfortunately only represented by rather small fragments, uses large fronds of palm, trilobate leaves or double-cone motives boldly silhouetted in a flat wash on a finely-hatched ground. In these pieces there is a strong tendency to divide the circular ground into three fields, each containing a complete unit of the design. The effect is singularly powerful. Less striking than this first style, although capable of considerable delicacy of effect, is one in which fine radiating stems bear cone-shaped leaves and trefoils against a background of dots (1), or another in which groups of tapering strokes are arranged within a palm border composed of similar strokes. The small bowl on Plate 83B is a coarser variant of this manner. Far less attractive than these is a mode of painting employing lines, cross-hatching, dots and roughly drawn rings in designs of no great originality or power.

The dating of Nabataean pottery has not been established within any but the broadest limits (approximately 100 B.C. until at least the second century A.D. or later), and until archaeology provides further evidence, it will not be possible to trace the evolution of the styles of painting which decorate it. It is evident, however, from the frequent use of the palm-frond and the cone-shaped leaf which, with its background of berries, so closely resembles the classical ivy motif (2), that once again on this 'native' pottery the elements of Greco-Roman art have undergone a transformation resulting in unexpected beauties.

Of a more conventional character is the flagon seen on Plate 83A, a piece belonging to no identified class of wares, but a reminder that the capacity to produce painted pottery was not entirely dead at this period in the Eastern Mediterranean.

Much has been said in the course of this book concerning the imitation of metalwork in pottery. Such imitations on Roman pottery were normally confined to the copying of the 'repoussé' technique used for obtaining relief-designs, and to the production of a surface suggesting metal in a general way. A more direct attempt to obtain a specifically metallic finish, however, is seen in a class of pottery coated with a wash containing innumerable specks of yellow mica, and thus given an appearance resembling bronze. This pottery, the shapes of which include jars, narrow-necked jugs, and bowls, appears to have been

---

(1) *Plate* 82A; (2) *Plate* 82A.

made in GAUL and the RHINELAND, although examples of it have been found in England (1).

   *   *   *   *   *   *

The pottery hitherto described in this chapter has been selected mainly on account of the interest of its ornamentation, artistically and technically. This emphasis, however, should not be permitted to distort the true picture of Roman pottery as a whole (if one can speak of such a thing) and to obscure the fact that for every piece of decorated ware there are many whose sole aesthetic claim resides in their form (2). Nor are these pieces necessarily of the finer fabrics. The simplest commercial containers, such as the innumerable amphorae used for the export and storage of wine or oil, whether plain (3) or inscribed in beautiful carefree script with a note of the contents (4), illustrate the formal virtues of freely-thrown pottery where there is mass-production without machinery. The cheapest kitchen crockery is endowed with qualities other than its mere utility, whether it be the simple mortar, made with a grog-roughened internal surface (5), or the pierced strainer thought to have been used for making small cheeses; the cooking-bowl or the storage jar (6). A variety of objects made for cult purposes, although of the cheapest fabrics, call forth the potter's cunning in a skilful exploitation of clay qualities (7). Nor were these formal virtues limited to the Northern Provinces of the Empire (8). Excellence of form in pottery, however humble the utensil, is not the sole prerogative of any one race of potters. To this truth the catholicity of Rome pays ample tribute.

_____

(1) *Plates* 84, 85. (2) *Plates* 86, 87, 90A, 91A; (3) *Plate* 88; (4) *Plate* 89; (5) *Plate* 93; (6) *Plate* 96; (7) *Plates* 90B, 91B, 92; (8) *Plates* 94, 95.

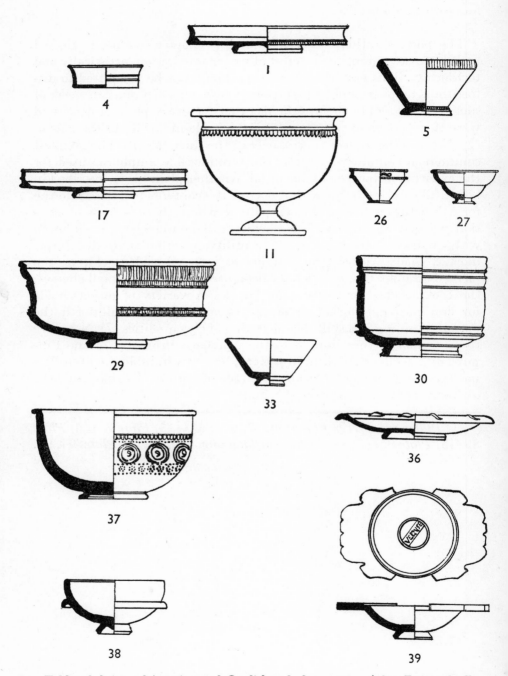

Table of shapes of Arretine and Gaulish red-gloss pottery (after Dragendorff).
The numerical series is that followed in the captions to the plates.

BIBLIOGRAPHY

Note: The books and articles on Roman pottery are legion. In this brief bibliography mainly the more recent literature is indicated. Many of these works themselves contain comprehensive bibliographies. Articles have in the main been omitted unless of particular importance.

GENERAL

H. B. Walters, *History of Ancient Pottery*, London (1905), Vol. II, pp. 430–555.

H. B. Walters, *Catalogue of the Roman Pottery in the Departments of Antiquities, British Museum*, London (1908).

F. Behn, *Römische Keramik . . .*, Mainz (1910).

CHAPTER 2

Howard Comfort, 'Terra Sigillata', in Pauly-Wissowa, *Real-Encyclopädie der classischen Altertumswissenschaft*, Supplementband VII (1950), cols. 1295–1352.

1. *Technique*

T. Schumann, '*Oberflächenverzierung in der antiken Töpferkunst . . .*', *Berichte der deutschen Ceramischen Gesellschaft*, Bd. 23, Heft 11 (November, 1942), pp. 408–26.

E. F. Prins de Jong and A. J. Rijken, 'Surface Decoration on Terra Sigillata . . .', *American Ceramic Society Bulletin*, Vol. 25, No. 1 (1946), pp. 5–7.

2. *Near Eastern Forerunners of Arretine, etc.*

F. Courby, *Les Vases grecs à reliefs*, Paris (1922).

M. Rostovtzeff, *The Social and Economic History of the Hellenistic World*, Oxford (1941), III, pp. 1406; 1445–6.

Frederick O. Waagé, 'Hellenistic and Roman Tableware of North Syria', in Princeton University, *Antioch-on-the-Orontes*, IV, Part I, *Ceramics and Islamic Coins*, Princeton (1948), pp. 1–43.

J. H. Iliffe 'Sigillata Wares in the Near East' (I and II), *Quarterly of the Department of Antiquities in Palestine*, VI, pp. 1–50, and IX, pp. 31–76.

Frances Follin Jones, in (ed.) Hetty Goldman, *Excavations at Gözlü Kule, Tarsus*, I (*The Hellenistic and Roman Periods*), Princeton (1950), pp. 172 ff.

3. *Italy*

A. Oxé, 'Römisch-italische Beziehungen der früharretinischen Relief-gefässe', *Bonner Jahrbücher* (1933), pp. 81–98.

A. Oxé, *Arretinische Reliefgefässe vom Rhein* (*Materialien zur römischgermanischen Keramik*, V), Frankfurt-am-Main (1933).

Corpus Vasorum Antiquorum: U.S.A., Metropolitan Museum of Art, New York, fasc. 1, *Arretine Relief Ware*, by Christine Alexander (1943).

H. Dragendorff (ed. C. Watzinger), *Arretinische Reliefkeramik*, Reutlingen (1948).

4. *Gaul*

F. Oswald and T. D. Pryce, *An Introduction to the Study of Terra Sigillata treated from a Chronological Standpoint*, London (1920).

F. Oswald, *Index of Potters' Stamps on Terra Sigillata*, published by the author, East Bridgford (1931).

F. Hermet, *La Graufesenque*, 2 vols., Paris (1934).

H. Ricken, *Die Bilderschüsseln der römischen Töpfer von Rheinzabern*, Darmstadt (1942).

5. *Late Roman Wares*

Frederick O. Waagé, *op. cit.*, pp. 43–58.

J. H. Iliffe, *loc. cit.*

Dorothy H. Cox, *The Greek and Roman Pottery* (*The Excavations at Dura-Europos, Final Report*, IV, Part I, fasc. 2), New Haven, U.S.A. (1949), pp. 14–16.

Frances Follin Jones, *op. cit.*, pp. 203–6.

CHAPTER 3

1. *Lead-glazed Wares*

a. Asia Minor, South Russia, etc.

R. Zahn, 'Glasierte Tongefässe im Antiquarium', *Amtliche Berichte aus den königlichen Kunstsammlungen* (Berlin), XXXV (1914), cols. 277–314.

R. Zahn, '*ΚΤΩ ΧΡΩ*: Glasierter Tonbecher im Berliner Antiquarium', 81 *Winckelmannsprogramm*, Berlin (1923).

M. Rostovtzeff, *op. cit.*, II, pp. 1010–11; III, p. 1582.

Frances Follin Jones, *op. cit.*, pp. 191–6.

Frances Follin Jones, '*Rhosica Vasa*', *American Journal of Archaeology*, XLIX (1945), pp. 45–51.

b. Gaul, the Northern Provinces, etc.

F. Behn, *op. cit.*, pp. 175–85.

E. M. Jope, 'Roman Lead-Glazed Pottery in Britain', *The Archaeological News Letter* (May, 1950), pp. 199–202.

BIBLIOGRAPHY

2. *Glazed Quartz Frit Ware*

H. Wallis, *Egyptian Ceramic Art: the MacGregor Collection*, London (1898).

W. M. Flinders Petrie, *Memphis I*, London (1909).

A. Lucas, 'Glazed Ware in Egypt, India and Mesopotamia', *Journal of Egyptian Archaeology*, XXII, Part II (1936), pp. 141–64.

M. Rostovtzeff, *op. cit.*, III, p. 1407.

3. *Alkaline-glazed Wares*

a. Mesopotamia and Syria

Neilson C. Debevoise, *Parthian Pottery from Seleucia on the Tigris*, Ann Arbor (1934).

R. Ettinghausen, 'Parthian and Sassanian Pottery', in A. U. Pope (ed.) *A Survey of Persian Art*, Oxford (1938), Vol. I, pp. 646–64.

M. Rostovtzeff, *op. cit.*, II, p. 1209; III, p. 1622.

Nicholas Toll, *The Green Glazed Pottery* (*The Excavations at Dura-Europos Final Report*, IV, Part I, fascicule 1), New Haven, U.S.A. (1943).

b. Gaul

Pro Nervia, IV (1928), p. 74.

CHAPTER 4

1. *Britain*

a. General

R. G. Collingwood, *The Archaeology of Roman Britain*, Chap. XIV ('Coarse Pottery'), London (1930), pp. 216–42.

British Museum, *A Guide to the Antiquities of Roman Britain*, by Reginald A. Smith, London (1922), pp. 112 ff.; and *Antiquities of Roman Britain*, by J. W. Brailsford, London (1951), pp. 31 ff.

C. F. C. Hawkes and M. R. Hull, *Camulodunum: first Report on the Excavations at Colchester* 1930–39, Oxford (1947).[1]

R. E. M. Wheeler and T. V. Wheeler, *Verulamium: a Belgic and two Roman Cities*, Oxford (1936).[1]

K. M. Kenyon, *Excavations at the Jewry Wall Site, Leicester*, Oxford (1948).[1]

b. Castor ware

M. V. Taylor, 'Romano-British Huntingdonshire', in *Victoria County History of . . . Huntingdonshire*, London (1926), pp. 219 ff.

[1] These titles are chosen, as covering a wide range of British-found wares, from amongst the numerous important excavation reports published by the Society of Antiquaries of London.

c. New Forest ware

Heywood Sumner, *Excavations in New Forest Pottery Sites* . . ., London (1927).

2. *Germany and Gaul*[1]

E. Ritterling, *Das frührömische Lager bei Hofheim im Taunus*, Wiesbaden (1913).

F. Oelmann, *Die Keramik des Kastells Niederbieber*, Frankfurt-am-Main (1914).

E. Gose, *Gefässtypen der römischen Keramik im Rheinland*, Kevelaer (1950).

G. Chenet, *La Céramique Gallo-Romaine d'Argonne du IVe siècle* . . . Macon (1941).

3. *Nubia*

C. Leonard Woolley and D. Randall-Maciver, *Karanòg: the Romano-Nubian Cemetery*, 2 vols., Philadelphia (1910).

F. Ll. Griffith, 'Oxford Excavations in Nubia', *University of Liverpool Annals of Archaeology and Anthropology*, XI (1924), pp. 115–25, 141–80; XII (1925), pp. 57–172.

4. *Nabatene*

Grace M. Crowfoot, 'The Nabataean Ware of Sbaita', *Palestine Exploration Fund Quarterly* (1936), pp. 14–27.

G. and A. Horsfield, 'Sela-Petra, the Rock of Edom and Nabatene', *Quarterly of the Department of Antiquities in Palestine*, VII (1938), pp. 1–42; VIII (1938–9), pp. 87–115; IX (1938–42), pp. 113–204.

[1] The first two works cited are old, but important, reports covering pottery of the earlier and later periods respectively.

INDEX

INDEX

Tschandarli, red-gloss pottery manufactured at, 9; lead-glazed pottery
manufactured at, 24

Umbria, 10, 11, 12
Upchurch, 33
Uruk. See Warka

Vandals, 22
Vasari, 5

'Venus Anadyomene', 29
Vesuvius, eruption of, 17
Vichy, 18; lead-glazed pottery manu-
factured at, 26
Vorus(?), potter, **8B**

Walters, H. B., 1, 3
Warka, alkaline-glazed pottery manu-
factured at, 30
Witham shield, 35

1. *Dish of Eastern fabric ('Pergamene') with stamped and rouletted decoration. Found at Samaria-Sebaste. About* 25 B.C. *Diam. app.* $11\frac{1}{8}$ *in. Courtesy The Joint Expedition to Samaria. See page* 7

2. *Bowl with moulded relief-decoration. Found in Italy.*
Italy or perhaps Alexandria. Probably 2nd century B.C. *Diam. 6 in.*
British Museum (G. & R.). See page 10

3. *Bowl with moulded relief-decoration and mark of the potter
L. Appius. Found, and made, in Italy. 2nd–1st century* B.C.
Diam. 4½ *in.*
British Museum (G. & R.). *See page* 11

4A. *Footed bowl ('crater') from Capua, with reliefs of the Seasons.*
Marked 'ATE' for 'ATEI'. Italy, factory of CN. ATEIUS. *About* 10–5 B.C.
Ht. $7\frac{1}{2}$ *in.*
British Museum (G. & R.). *See page* 14
4B. *Mould for an Arretine bowl, with 'kalathiskos' dancers. Signed by*
Pilemo as workman in the Perennius factory. About 25–10 B.C.
Diam. $7\frac{1}{4}$ *in.*
Metropolitan Museum of Art, New York. See pages 12, 13, 14

5A. *Footed bowl ('crater') from Mainz. Marked 'ATEI'. Italy, factory of* CN. ATEIUS. *About* 10–5 B.C. *Ht.* 5⅗ *in.*
Römisch-Germanisches Zentralmuseum, Mainz. See page 15
5B. *Mould for an Arretine bowl. Signed by Pantagathus as a workman in the Rasinius factory. About* 10 B.C.–A.D. 10. *Diam.* 6 7/16 *in.*
Metropolitan Museum of Art, New York. See pages 13, 14

6. *Cup. Perhaps made in the workshop of M. Perennius Bargathes at Arretium. About* 10–15 A.D. *Ht.* $7\frac{3}{16}$ *in.*
Metropolitan Museum of Art, New York. See page 14

7A. *Bowl (Form 30) with moulded decoration. Found at Sandy,*
Bedfordshire. La Graufesenque, about 50 A.D. Ht. 4¾ in.
British Museum (B. & M.). See pages 16, 18
7B. *Bowl (Form 29) with moulded and rouletted decoration. Found in*
London. La Graufesenque. 1st century A.D. Diam. 9¾ in.
British Museum (B. & M.). See pages 18, 21

8A. *Cup (Form 26) with rouletted decoration and stamp of the potter*
CN. ATEIUS. *Found at Colchester. Made in Italy or at an affiliated
Rhenish factory. Early 1st century* A.D. *Ht. 3 in.*
Colchester & Essex Museum, Colchester. See page 15

8B. *Dish (Form 1) with the stamp of the potter* (?) *Vorus. Found at
Vaison, in Provence. Italian; Augustan. Diam.* $6\frac{1}{2}$ *in.*
British Museum (G. & R.). *See page 15*

9A. *Cup (Form 26), from Olbia. Near Eastern fabric (perhaps 'Pergamene'); first half of the 1st century* A.D. *Diam.* $4\frac{1}{3}$ *in.*
Rijksmuseum van Oudheden te Leiden. See page 7

9B. *Dish (Form 17) with the stamp of the potter* PHILOSUS (? *for* PILOSUS). *Found near Ventimiglia. Made in South Gaul; probably 2nd quarter of 1st century* A.D. *Diam.* $6\frac{7}{8}$ *in.*
Victoria & Albert Museum. See page 21

10A. *Cup (Form 33) with the stamp of the potter Butturrus. Found at
Harpenden. Lezoux; mid-2nd century* A.D. *Diam.* 4⅛ *in.*
British Museum (B. & M.). See page 21

10B. *Dish with marbled decoration, and stamp of the potter Ardanus,
found at Arles. La Graufesenque; mid-1st century* A.D.
Diam. 5⅛ *in.*
British Museum (G. & R.). See page 20

11A. *Cup (Form 27) with stamp of the workshop of the potter Secundus.*
Found in Suffolk Lane, London. La Graufesenque; third quarter of the
1st century A.D. *Diam.* 4⅜ *in.*
British Museum (B. & M.). See page 21
11B. *Mortarium-shaped bowl. Found at Cologne. South Gaul; mid-1st*
century A.D. *Diam.* 6¾ *in.*
British Museum (G. & R.). See page 21

12A. *Bowl (Form 37) with moulded decoration and the stamp of the*
potter Paternus. Found at Wingham, Kent.
Lezoux; mid-2nd century A.D. *Ht. 5¾ in.*
British Museum (B. & M.). See page 19
12B. *Tray (Form 39) with slip-decoration. Found at Bonn. Eastern*
Gaul; 2nd century A.D. *Length 6½ in.*
Rheinisches Landesmuseum, Bonn. See page 19

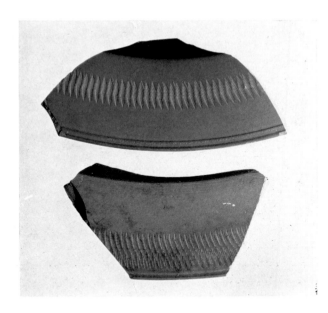

13A. *Bowl (Form 37) with rouletted decoration. Found at Heddernheim.*
Eastern Gaul; 2nd century A.D. *Diam.* $9\frac{1}{4}$ *in.*
British Museum (G. & R.). *See page* 20
13B. *Rim-fragments of bowls, with rouletted decoration. Found at*
Dura-Europos. 'Late A' ware. Probably second quarter of the 3rd
century A.D.
Yale University Art Gallery. See page 22

14. *Flagon with incised decoration. Found at Cologne. Probably
Rheinzabern or Trèves; 3rd century* A.D. *Ht. 6 in.
Rheinisches Landesmuseum, Bonn. See page* 20

15. *Cup with incised decoration. Found at Araines. Probably Lezoux;*
mid-2nd century A.D. *Ht.* $3\frac{3}{4}$ *in.*
Ashmolean Museum, Oxford. See page 20

16. *Jar decorated with overlapping applied scales. Found at Cologne.*
Gaul; second half of 1st century A.D. *Ht.* $4\frac{3}{8}$ *in.*
Victoria and Albert Museum. Crown Copyright. See page 23

17. *Barrel-shaped jar with overlapping applied scales. Found at Bonn.*
Probably made in the Rhineland; 2nd century A.D. *Ht.* $5\frac{1}{8}$ *in.*
Rheinisches Landesmuseum, Bonn. See page 19

18. *Flagon with slip-decoration. Found at Olbia, South Russia.*
Asia Minor; 1st century A.D. *Ht.* $6\frac{1}{4}$ *in.*
Rijksmuseum van Oudheden te Leiden. See page 23

19. *Beaker with slip-decoration. Found in the Rhineland. Probably Rheinzabern; 3rd century* A.D. *Ht.* $6\frac{1}{4}$ *in. British Museum* (G. & R.). *See page* 19

20. *Globular beaker (Form 54) with slip-decoration. Found at Bonn.*
Probably Rheinzabern; about 150–250 A.D. *Ht.* 5 *in.*
Rheinisches Landesmuseum, Bonn. See page 19

21. *Bowl (handle broken off), with slip-decoration. Found at Mainz.*
Probably Rheinzabern; about 150–250 A.D. *Diam.* $5\frac{1}{8}$ *in.*
Römisch-Germanisches Zentralmuseum, Mainz. See page 19

22A. *Beaker with rouletted and incised decoration. Found near Cologne.*
Gaul; 1st half of 1st century A.D. *Ht. 5⅝ in.*
Victoria & Albert Museum. See page 23
22B. *Dish with stamped decoration, from Tunis. Near Eastern fabric*
('Late B'); probably 4th century A.D. *Diam. 12¾ in.*
Rijksmuseum van Oudheden te Leiden. See page 21

23A. *Jug with rouletted decoration, from Carthage. Near Eastern fabric (probably 'Late B'); probably 3rd century* A.D. *Ht.* $3\frac{1}{2}$ *in. Rijksmuseum van Oudheden te Leiden. See page 21*

23B. *Dish with stamped decoration, from Tunis. Near Eastern fabric ('Late B'); probably 4th century* A.D. *Diam.* $13\frac{1}{2}$ *in. Rijksmuseum van Oudheden te Leiden. See page 21*

24A. *Bowl with rouletted decoration, perhaps found at Vulci. Near Eastern fabric ('Late B'); probably 2nd century* A.D. *Diam.* $9\frac{1}{4}$ *in. Vatican Museum. See page* 21

24B. *Dish with slip-decoration, from Sousse. Near Eastern fabric ('Late B'); 2nd or 3rd century* A.D. *Diam.* $7\frac{3}{5}$ *in. Rijksmuseum van Oudheden te Leiden. See page* 21

25A. *Dish, from Tunisia. Near Eastern fabric ('Late A'); 3rd or 4th century* A.D. *Diam.* $8\frac{3}{4}$ *in.*
Rijksmuseum van Oudheden te Leiden. See page 22

25B. *Dish with foot-print stamp, from Olbia. Near Eastern fabric (perhaps 'Pergamene'); 1st century* A.D. *Diam.* $7\frac{7}{8}$ *in.*
Rijksmuseum van Oudheden te Leiden. See page 7

26. *Flask, found at Osuna, near Seville. Probably La Graufesenque;*
1st century A.D. *Ht. 7 in.*
The Hispanic Society of America, New York. See page 21

27. *Amphora, green lead-glazed earthenware. Asia Minor.*
1st century B.C. *or* A.D. *Ht.* $10\frac{7}{16}$ *in.*
Metropolitan Museum of Art, New York. See page 25

28A. *Cup (scyphus), yellowish-brown lead-glazed earthenware, with
reliefs perhaps referring to the Bacchic cult. Asia Minor.
1st century* B.C. *or* A.D. *Ht.* 2⅞ *in.*
See page 24

28B. *Cup, lead-glazed earthenware, green outside and brownish-yellow
inside. Asia Minor. 1st century* B.C. *or* A.D. *Ht.* 3⅞ *in. See page 25*
Courtesy of the Museum of Fine Arts, Boston.

29A. *Ink-well, green lead-glazed earthenware. Reputedly found at Hama, Syria. Asia Minor. 1st century* B.C. *or* A.D. *Ht.* $2\frac{3}{16}$ *in. Metropolitan Museum of Art, New York. See page 25*

29B. *Beaker, green lead-glazed earthenware with trailed slip decoration. Found, and perhaps made, in South Russia. 1st century* B.C. *or* A.D. *Ht. 4 in. Staatlichen Museen, Berlin. See page 25*

30A. *Jug, green lead-glazed earthenware, with slip-decoration. Found in
a tomb at Olbia, South Russia. Probably South Russia.
1st century* B.C. *or* A.D. *Ht.* $8\frac{9}{16}$ *in.*
Metropolitan Museum of Art, New York. See page 25
30B. *Lamp, green lead-glazed earthenware with figures of gladiators.
Found in a tomb at Pozzuoli. Italy; late 1st century* A.D. *Length* $5\frac{1}{8}$*in.*
Ashmolean Museum, Oxford. See page 26

31A. *Beaker (modiolus), green lead-glazed earthenware, with moulded and slip-decoration in white and red clays. Found in Southern Thrace. Probably South Russia. 1st century* B.C. *or* A.D. *Ht.* $6\frac{1}{8}$ *in. Staatlichen Museen, Berlin. See page 25*

31B. *Jug (askos), brown and green lead-glazed earthenware. Found, and probably made, in Italy. 1st century* A.D. *Ht.* $5\frac{1}{3}$ *in. Musée du Louvre, Paris. See page 26*

32. *Jug, greenish-yellow lead-glazed earthenware. Found at Colchester.*
St. Rémy-en-Rollat. Middle of 1st century A.D. *Ht.* $7\frac{1}{4}$ *in.*
Colchester and Essex Museum, Colchester. See page 26

33A and B. *Unguent-flasks in the form of a hare and an ibex, yellowish lead-glazed earthenware. Found at Colchester. St. Rémy-en-Rollat. Middle of 1st century A.D. Hts. 3 in. and 4¼ in. Colchester and Essex Museum, Colchester. See page 26*

34. *Jug, green lead-glazed earthenware. Found in a grave at Trier with a coin of Hadrian. Lezoux or Cologne. Middle or end of 2nd century* A.D. *Ht.* 11⅝ *in.*
Landesmuseum, Trier. See page 26

35. 'Puzzle-jug', dark-green lead-glazed earthenware. Found at Dunapentele, Hungary. Pannonia. 3rd–4th century A.D. Ht. 9 in. Römisch-Germanisches Zentralmuseum, Mainz. See page 26

36. *Jug, green lead-glazed earthenware with incised decoration. Found,
and probably made, in Cologne. First half of 3rd century* A.D.
Ht. 8¼ *in.*
Römisch-Germanisches Museum, Cologne. See page 26

37. *Bottle-jug, green lead-glazed earthenware with impressed decoration. Probably found and made in Cologne. Probably 3rd century* A.D. *Ht.* 10¼ *in.*
Römisch-Germanisches Museum, Cologne. See page 26

38A. *Beaker, green lead-glazed earthenware with slip-decoration. Found in Bonn. Probably Cologne. Late 2nd or 3rd century* A.D. *Ht. 4 in.*
Rheinisches Landesmuseum, Bonn. See page 26
38B. *Jar, greyish-green lead-glazed earthenware. Found in Cambridge. Rhineland or perhaps Britain. Second half of 2nd century* A.D. *Ht. 5 in.*
University Museum of Archaeology and Ethnology, Cambridge.
See page 26

39A. *Dish (restored), green lead-glazed earthenware with slip-decoration. Found in Bonn. Probably Cologne. Late 2nd or 3rd century* A.D. *Diam.* 4¼ *in.*
Rheinisches Landesmuseum, Bonn. See page 26

39B. *Jar, glazed quartz frit ware with carved decoration. Egypt. 3rd century* B.C. *or later. Ht.* 4¾ *in.*
Kelekian Collection. Crown Copyright. See page 28

40. *Covered vase, turquoise-glazed quartz frit ware with incised
decoration. Egypt, perhaps Memphis. Probably 1st century* A.D.
Ht. 6¾ *in.*
Museum für Kunst und Gewerbe, Hamburg. See page 29

41. *Vase, glazed quartz frit ware with applied decoration. Found at
Hawara. Egypt. 1st or 2nd century* A.D. *Ht.* 6¾ *in.
Musée du Louvre, Paris. See page 28*

42A. *Plate, glazed quartz frit ware with design painted in manganese-brown and turquoise on a white ground. Egypt, perhaps Memphis. Probably 1st century* A.D. *Diam.* $8\frac{1}{2}$ *in. Victoria & Albert Museum. Crown Copyright. See page 28*

42B. *Portrait-bust of the Emperor Tiberius, blue-glazed quartz frit ware. Egypt. About 30* A.D. *Ht.* $3\frac{1}{2}$ *in. Cabinet des Médailles, Bibliothèque Nationale, Paris. See page 29*

43A. *Vase, turquoise-glazed quartz frit ware with carved decoration.*
Egypt, perhaps Memphis. Probably 1st century A.D. *Ht. 7½ in.*
Eton College Museum. See page 28

43B. *Head of Hercules, from a vessel. Blue- and green-glazed quartz*
frit ware, the eyes manganese-purple. Found at Kom-Wushim, Fayoum.
Egypt. 1st or 2nd century A.D. *Ht. 3¾ in.*
Victoria and Albert Museum. See page 29

44. *Two-handled vase, blue-green alkaline-glazed pottery. Reputedly found at Salemiyeh, Syria. Probably Western Mesopotamia. 1st century* B.C. *or* A.D. *Ht.* $14\frac{1}{8}$ *in. Metropolitan Museum of Art, New York. See page* 30

45. *Two-handled vase, blue-green alkaline-glazed pottery. Found, and probably made, at Dura-Europos, Mesopotamia. 1st century* A.D. *Ht. 10½ in.*
Yale University Art Gallery. See page 30

46. *Two-handled vase, originally green alkaline-glazed pottery.*
Mesopotamia. 1st–3rd century A.D. *Ht.* 11½ *in.*
Sir Ernest Debenham Collection. See page 30

47. *Vase, bluish alkaline-glazed pottery. Found, and probably made, at Dura-Europos, Mesopotamia. 2nd–3rd century* A.D. *Ht.* 13$\frac{1}{8}$ *in. Yale University Art Gallery. See page* 30

48. *Jar of greyish-black earthenware with burnished and incised
decoration. Found at Water Newton, Huntingdon. Second half of
1st century* A.D. *Ht.* $5\frac{7}{8}$ *in.*
Victoria & Albert Museum. Crown Copyright. See pages 33, 34

49. *'Poppy-head' beaker with glossy black surface slip-decorated with bands of dots. Mid-2nd century* A.D. *Ht.* 6½ *in.*
Victoria & Albert Museum. See page 34

50. *Cooking-jar of grey clay with scored decoration. Found at Colchester. Late 1st century* A.D. *Ht.* 11½ *in. Colchester and Essex Museum, Colchester. See page* 34

51. *Storage-jar of grey clay with burnished and incised decoration.
Found at Colchester. Late 3rd or 4th century* A.D. *Ht.* 11½ *in.
Colchester and Essex Museum, Colchester. See page* 34

52. *Jar with glossy black surface and incised decoration. Found at
Colchester. Probably British; second half of 1st century* A.D. *Ht. 12 in.
Colchester and Essex Museum, Colchester. See page* 34

53. *Beaker of dark-grey clay, with rouletted decoration. Found at Colchester. Probably British; 2nd half of 1st century* A.D. *Ht.* $8\frac{1}{4}$ *in. Colchester and Essex Museum, Colchester. See page* 34

54. *Bowl of buff clay, with applied decoration. Found near Cologne.*
Probably Rhenish, middle of 1st century A.D. *Diam.* 4 *in.*
Victoria & Albert Museum. See page 34

55. *Cup of orange-coated pinkish-buff clay, with applied slip-decora-*
tion. Found near Ventimiglia. Probably South Gaulish; middle of
1st century A.D. *Ht.* $2\frac{7}{8}$ *in.*
Victoria & Albert Museum. See page 34

56. *Bowl of pink clay with slip-decoration in white and pink. Found at Koptos, Upper Egypt. Egyptian; probably 1st century* A.D. *Ht.* $4\frac{3}{4}$ *in. Victoria & Albert Museum. See page 34*

57. *Jar of greyish-buff clay with slip-decoration of brown dots. Found at Snape Abbey, Suffolk. Perhaps British; late 1st century* A.D. *Ht. 4 in. British Museum (B. & M.). See page 34*

58. *Jar of dark-coated grey clay with raised slip-decoration ('rustic ware'). Found at York. North British; second half of 1st century* A.D. *Ht. 6½ in.*
Yorkshire Museum, York. See page 34

59. *Jar of dark-coated grey clay with raised slip-decoration ('rustic ware'). Found at York. North British; second half of 1st century* A.D. *Ht.* 5⅜ *in.*
Yorkshire Museum, York. See page 34

60. *Beaker with glossy black surface, decorated with trailed slip. Found at Silchester. Probably Gaulish; 3rd century* A.D. *Ht. 5 in. Reading Museum. See page 35*

61. *Beaker of dark-coated light clay decorated with trailed slip.*
British (Castor ware); late 2nd or 3rd century A.D. *Ht.* 5⅝ *in.*
Royal Ontario Museum of Archaeology, Toronto. See page 35

62. *'Hunt cup' of dark-coated light clay decorated with trailed slip.*
British (Castor ware); late 2nd or 3rd century A.D. *Ht. 4 in.*
Yorkshire Museum, York. See page 35

63. *'Hunt cup' of dark-coated light clay decorated with trailed slip.
British (Castor ware); late 2nd or 3rd century* A.D. *Ht.* $5\frac{7}{16}$ *in.
Yorkshire Museum, York. See page 35*

64. *Cup and cover of dark-coated light clay decorated with trailed Slip.*
Probably British (Castor ware); late 2nd century A.D. *Ht.* $3\frac{3}{4}$ *in.*
Colchester and Essex Museum, Colchester. See page 35

65. *Beaker of dark-coated light clay decorated with trailed slip and incised with the names of the gladiators represented (the 'Colchester vase'). Probably British (Castor ware); late 2nd century* A.D. *Ht.* 8½ *in. Colchester and Essex Museum, Colchester. See page 35*

66A. *Beaker of dark-coated light clay decorated with trailed slip.*
British (Castor ware); late 2nd or 3rd century A.D.
Yorkshire Museum, York. See page 35

66B. *Bowl of dark-coated light clay, with incised and rouletted decora-*
tion. Probably Argonne region; 4th century A.D. *Diam.* $5\frac{3}{4}$ *in.*
British Museum (G. & R.). See page 35

67A. *Beaker of dark-coated light clay, with incised and rouletted*
decoration. From Meix-Tiercelin (Marne).
Argonne region; 4th century A.D. *Ht.* $5\frac{1}{2}$ *in.*
British Museum (G. & R.). See page 35

67B. *Bowl of dark-coated light clay, with rouletted decoration. Probably*
Argonne region; 4th century A.D. *Diam.* $4\frac{3}{4}$ *in.*
British Museum (G. & R.). See page 35

68. *Beaker of dark-coated grey earthenware with indentations.*
Probably found and made in the New Forest;
late 3rd or 4th century A.D. *Ht.* 5¾ *in.*
Victoria & Albert Museum. See page 36

69. *Beaker of dark-coated light clay, with indentations and scale-ornament. Found at Water Newton. British (Castor ware); late 3rd or early 4th century* A.D. *Ht.* $7\frac{1}{2}$ *in.*
University Museum of Archaeology and Ethnology, Cambridge.

See page 35

70. *Beaker of dark-coated light clay, decorated with rouletting and trailed white slip. Found at Duston, Northants. British (Castor ware); 1st half of 3rd century* A.D. *Ht.* $4\frac{1}{2}$ *in.*
British Museum (G. & R.). *See page* 35

71. *Beaker of dark-coated earthenware decorated with trailed white slip. Found at Bonn. Rhenish; late 2nd or early 3rd century* A.D. *Ht.* $4\frac{9}{10}$ *in.*
Rheinisches Landesmuseum, Bonn. See page 36

72. *Beaker of dark-coated earthenware decorated with rouletting and trailed white slip. 'Vincote' ('Success to you'). Found at Colchester. British (Castor ware); 3rd century* A.D. *Ht. 4 in.*
Colchester and Essex Museum, Colchester. See pages 35, 36

73. *Jug of dark-coated red earthenware decorated with rouletting and trailed white and brownish-red slip.* 'SVME' (*'Take'*). *Found in Cologne. Rhenish (probably Trier); early 3rd century* A.D. *Ht.* 10½ *in. Römisch-Germanisches Museum, Cologne. See page* 36

74. *Flagon, dark earthenware with trailed white slip decoration. Found and made in the New Forest; early 4th century* A.D. *Ht.* 6⅝ *in. British Museum* (B. & M.). *See page* 36

75. *Bottle, dark earthenware with trailed white slip decoration. Found and made in the New Forest; 4th century* A.D. *Ht. 5 in.*
British Museum (B. & M.). *See page* 36

76. *Jug of yellowish earthenware, with painting in dark red-brown.*
Found at Pallien, near Trier. Rhenish (Speicher-in-der-Eifel);
4th century A.D. *Ht.* 9⅝ *in.*
Landesmuseum, Trier. See page 36

77. *Jug of buff earthenware, with painting in red. Found at Colchester:
probably made locally. 4th century* A.D. *Ht. 7½ in.
Colchester and Essex Museum, Colchester. See page* 36

78. *Flagon of yellow-coated pink earthenware painted in red and purple. Found at Faras. Nubian; 1st or 2nd century* A.D.
Ht. $7\frac{1}{4}$ in.
Ashmolean Museum, Oxford. See pages 36, 37

79. *Cup of buff earthenware painted in dark purple. Found at Faras.*
Nubian; 1st or 2nd century A.D. *Ht.* $4\frac{3}{8}$ *in.*
Ashmolean Museum, Oxford. See page 37

80. *Jar of buff-coated red earthenware, painted in purple and red.*
Found at Faras. Nubian; 1st or 2nd century A.D. *Ht. 10 in.*
Ashmolean Museum, Oxford. See page 37

81. *Jar of earthenware coated red-brown and painted in purplish-black.*
Egyptian ('Coptic'); 6th century A.D. *or later.*
Ht. approximately 14 in.
Kelekian Collection. Crown Copyright. See page 37

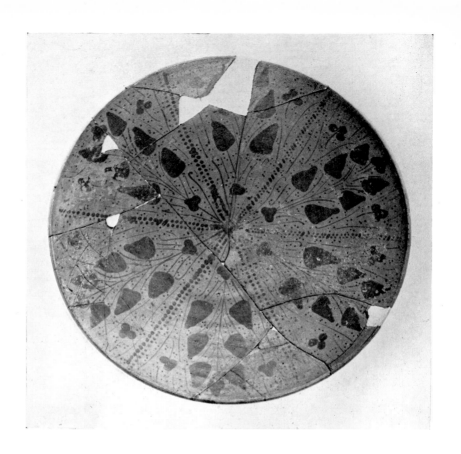

82A. *Bowl of thin pink-coated red earthenware, painted in dark brownish-red. Found at 'Amman, Transjordan. 'Nabataean'; probably 1st century* A.D. *Diam* $6\frac{4}{5}$ *in.*
Palestine Archaeological Museum, Jerusalem. See page 38
82B. *Jar of buff earthenware painted in red. Found at Colchester. Probably British; late 1st century* A.D. *Ht.* $3\frac{3}{4}$ *in.*
British Museum (B. & M.). See page 36

83A. *Flagon of reddish earthenware, painted in red. Found in Crete.*
Eastern Mediterranean; probably 1st century A.D. *Ht.* $6\frac{7}{10}$ *in.*
Rijksmuseum van Oudheden te Leiden. See page 38
83B. *Bowl of pink earthenware painted in dark-red. Found at Petra.*
'Nabataean'; 1st century B.C. *or* A.D. *Diam.* 4 *in.*
University Museum of Archaeology and Ethnology, Cambridge.
See page 38

84. *Jar of light-red earthenware dusted with mica. Found at Colchester.*
Gallo-Belgic; middle of 1st century A.D. *Ht.* $3\frac{1}{2}$ *in.*
British Museum (B. & M.). See pages 38, 39

85. *Jar of light-red clay dusted with mica. Marked* 'CAMARO. F (*ecit*)'
impressed. Found at Lincoln. Gallo-Belgic; 3rd quarter of
1st century A.D. *Ht.* 6½ *in.*
British Museum (B. & M.). *See pages* 38, 39

86. *Beaker of buff clay, with rouletted decoration. Found at Sandy,*
Beds. Probably British; late 2nd or 3rd century A.D. *Ht.* $5\frac{1}{4}$ *in.*
British Museum (B.& M.). See page 39

87. *Beaker of light drab clay, originally covered with dark coating. From Upchurch, Kent. Probably 1st or 2nd century* A.D. *Ht.* $3\frac{5}{8}$ *in. Royal Ontario Museum of Archaeology, Toronto. See pages 33, 39*

88. *Jar of buff earthenware, found at Pompeii. Probably Italian;
2nd or 3rd quarter of 1st century* A.D. *Ht.* 20½ *in.
Rijksmuseum van Oudheden te Leiden. See page* 39

89. *Wine amphora, of greyish earthenware, inscribed in red. Found at
Firka. Probably 5th century* A.D. *Ht.* 19¾ *in.
Ashmolean Museum, Oxford. See page* 39

90A. *Barrel-shaped costrel, of red earthenware with turned decoration.*
Perhaps British; 2nd or 3rd century A.D. *Ht. 5½ in.*
British Museum (B. & M.). See page 39
90B. *Frilled 'incense-bowl' for funerary purposes, of buff earthenware.*
Found at Colchester. British or Rhenish; probably late 1st or 2nd
century A.D. *Ht. 3¼ in.*
Colchester and Essex Museum, Colchester. See page 39

91A. *Bulbous beaker, of dark-coated earthenware, with rouletted decoration. Found in Cologne. Rhenish; 1st half of 3rd century* A.D. *Ht.* 3¾ *in.*
British Museum (G. & R.). See page 39

91B. *Triple drinking-vessel of reddish earthenware, probably symbolising Unity or Brotherhood. Found at Colchester. British; perhaps 2nd or 3rd century* A.D. *Ht.* 3¼ *in.*
Colchester and Essex Museum, Colchester. See page 39

92. 'Face-urn' of creamy earthenware, with stamped and applied
decoration: probably for votive purposes. Found at Colchester. Probably
Rhenish; 1st half of 2nd century A.D. Ht. 10½ in.
Colchester and Essex Museum, Colchester. See page 39

93. *Kitchen-mortar ('mortarium') of hard greyish-white earthenware,
for grinding food, the inner surface being lined with grit-particles.
British; 4th century* A.D. *Diam.* 10½ *in.*
Colchester and Essex Museum, Colchester. See page 39

94. *Cup of pinkish-orange earthenware, with incised decoration. Found near Ventimiglia. Probably South Gaulish; 1st century* A.D. *Ht.* $4\frac{1}{8}$ *in. Victoria and Albert Museum. See page* 39

95. *Bowl of red earthenware. Found, and probably made, in North Africa. Probably 3rd century* A.D. *Ht. approx.* $6\frac{1}{2}$ *in.*
Rijksmuseum van Oudheden te Leiden. See page 39

96. *Jar of red-surfaced earthenware, used as a cinerary urn. Found at Old Ford, London. Perhaps Gaulish; 1st century* A.D. *Ht. 1 ft.* $2\frac{1}{2}$ *in. British Museum* (B. & M.). *See page 39*